rollerskating

by
Gloria D. Miklowitz

tempo
books
GROSSET & DUNLAP
A Filmways Company
Publishers • New York

Photo Credits: Erik Haugaard, pages: vi, 3, 4, 6, 26, 36, 37, 40, 41, 42, 43, 44, 45, 46, 49, 50, 51, 52, 54, 56, 57, 58, 59, 60, 61, 62, 63, 65, 66, 69, 73, 80, 81, 86, 87, 88, 90, 92, 120, 123, 124, 125, 126, 127, 128, 129, 130, 134, 135, 136, 140, 141, 142, 144, 145, 146, 148, 150, 151, 153, 154, 155, 156, 157, 158, 159, 160

Library of Congress, pages: 8, 10, 13, 15, 16, 17, 21, 22

Boy Scouts of America, pages: 47, 48, 164, 166

Randall Harbuck, pages: 98, 115, 117

Nicki Armstrong, pages: 73, 113

Sure Grip International, pages: 75, 76 bottom

Roller Derby: 67

Pop Wheels: 74

Mattel: 78

Road Skates International: 72

Tom Jadwin: 114

Pamela Young: 96

Fred Dagher: 76 top

Illustrations courtesy of Chicago Roller Skate Company. Revised by Gary Brodsky.

Book Design by Elaine Golt Gongora

ROLLER SKATING

ACKNOWLEDGMENT

My sincerest appreciation to the following people who so generously gave me their time and help in the preparation of this book: Chris Baerg, skating instructor at Skate-O-Rama, Downey, California; Jerry Nista, owner of Skate-O-Rama; Fred Dagher, skater and enthusiast who introduced me to the skateboard parks; Suzanne Thomas, of Road Skates International; Harry Ball, Sure-Grip Skates; Joe Shevelson, Chicago Skates; and, of course, the Roller Skating Operators of America, in Lincoln, Nebraska.

contents

Along the boardwalk on a balmy day.

introduction

ARE THERE ANY other people in the world more in love with wheels than Americans?

Given the choice between walking and riding, Americans opt for wheels 98 percent of the time. We *roll* through life, on bikes, skateboards, motorcycles, in cars. And more recently, on eight wheels attached to our two feet—roller skates.

Roller skating's not all that new. It's been around a long time. Its popularity has been up (in the '40s) and down (in the '60s). But suddenly, now, heading into the '80s, the interest in roller skating is rocketing. Since 1970 the number of indoor roller rinks in the United States has tripled. Over 4,000 rinks cater to the skating crowds, with more being built each day. It's estimated that as many as 60 million Americans are into skating these days, from age two to eighty-two.

What's made roller skating so appealing now, a hundred years after it first became a sport in this country? *Wheels.* The same wheels that caused the skateboard craze. Attached now to skates, those wheels make all the difference in the world. Before, outdoor roller skating was only for young people. The hard, narrow wheels made for rough rides. Only a kid would put up with the spine-jolting, balance-testing rides over sidewalks pocked with cracks and holes.

Speed skaters at a competition.

Then came the wider, softer urethane wheels. They glide over the bumps, the asphalt roughness, through the sand and dirt, and the skater hardly notices. Suddenly, skating appeals to the 20-and-up crowds, as well as the young. Why jog, when skating gives as much exercise and is more fun?

These days mothers push baby carriages and shop in supermarkets while on skates. In Los Angeles, Linda Ronstadt skated to a lunch date with Governor Jerry Brown. In Minneapolis, the owner of Rolling Soles ties his shoes to his belt loops and takes off on skates. In San Francisco, a twenty-year-old mechanical engineer rolls off to his job seven miles away, dressed in suit and tie. And in Chicago, the president of the Stockbrokers Association rolls to and from work over lumpy sidewalks and bumper-to-bumper streets. Wearing blue and yellow "jogger" skates, he averages eight miles each way from his home in Evanston, through rain, snow, and

Competitive skaters start young.

Skating the skateboard parks.

dark of night. Why? Because he likes the "sense of power I get from scraping the sidewalk."

It's not just outdoors, along the bikeways and boardwalks, in the city streets and parks and skateboard parks that the change has come. There's a new attitude indoors, too, where rink skaters range from weekend-

recreation types to disco dance freaks and serious competitive skaters.

Twenty-six thousand skaters compete annually in artistic skating, speed skating, and roller hockey contests. They're able to do things even the best ice skaters only recently attempted. Natalie Dunn, three-time world

The disco scene.

freestyle skating champion says, "Just recently, only a few ice skaters could do triple jumps. Men did it first. Now Linda Fratianne is considered sensational because she can do them. But top roller skaters, men and women, have been doing triple jumps for years!"

The best skaters today no longer have to hang up their wheels at the age of twenty in order to go out and earn a living. For the first time in the history of roller skating, they have other choices. *They can make their living skating.* There's a new and growing demand for teachers. Each rink needs at least one and often several. But the most interesting development has been the call for skaters in the entertainment industry. Attractive boys and girls and men and women who know their way around on skates are getting paid—and well—to appear in fashion shows, in TV commercials, on TV programs, and in motion pictures.

Skaters are now asking, "If there's an Ice Capades, why not a Roller Skapades?" And indeed, why not? Roller skaters are every bit as graceful, inventive, and beautiful to watch as those on ice. The U.S. already has its Dorothy Hamill in Natalie Dunn, national and world artistic skater.

So, skating as a career need no longer be just a dream. It's for real. It's not only possible, it's happening here and now. But to get there, you've got to be the best.

ROLLER SKATING is about this old-new sport. It's for the outdoor and the indoor skater. For the guy or gal just starting out on skates at age two, or ten, or six times ten. And also, for the guy or gal whose feet feel weird without their wheels.

It's about skates, the kinds, the prices, and how to care for them, and about skating, how to do the basics and some of the fancier stuff. It's about requirements for scout badges and about competitions, and it's also about disco skating and skateboard park skating, and just plain rolling-along-in-the-park skating.

In 1865 William H. Fuller went "Round the World on Skates."

how it all began

No ONE REALLY knows who invented the first roller skates, but it was probably a Dutchman. This unknown inventor is thought to have been so crazy about ice skating that he couldn't stand the months when the ice in the canals melted, forcing him to put away his skates.

One hot summer's day about 250 years ago, dreaming of the figure eights he could be doing if only the canals were frozen, he got an idea. Why not put wheels on his shoes? Then, he could slide around on the pavements and roads of old Holland even if it wasn't winter.

And so, this clever Dutchman nailed some large wooden spools to strips of wood attached to his shoes, and off he went. His idea spread. Soon, people throughout Holland were converting their shoes and even their ice skates to roller skates.

History credits Joseph Merlin, not the Dutchman, as the first person to make a pair of roller skates. Merlin was born in Belgium. He became a musical instrument maker and mechanic. For a while he worked in France, but then went to England. There, some of his inventions were displayed in museums, including his own, a place called Merlin's Cave. One of his most unusual inventions was a pair of skates on wheels.

In 1760, Merlin was invited by a famous hostess to

A roller rink in the 1880's.

perform at a party in London. He arrived at the elegant home with his violin and wearing "a pair of skates contrived to run on small metallic wheels." As he rolled along among the guests, all went well—for a while. But not for long. Merlin's skates were designed so that changing direction wasn't possible. Worse still, he didn't know how to stop.

And so, poor Merlin sailed along on the ballroom floor, fiddling away on his violin and picking up speed, until—Wham!—he ran straight into a $2,000 mirror. According to a report written of that event, he "dashed it [the mirror] to atoms, broke his instrument to pieces, and wounded himself most severely."

Some sixty years later, in 1819, a Monsieur Petitbled took out the first patent for a roller skate. His device consisted of a wooden sole to which two, three, or four rollers were fitted, in a straight line. The rollers were all the same size and made of either copper, wood, or ivory. Petitbled claimed his skate was easy to control, but the truth was, it was almost impossible to skate any way except straight ahead.

A few years later a fruit merchant in London by the name of Robert John Tyers patented a skate with five wheels in a single line. It was described as "an apparatus to be attached to boots, shoes, and other covering for the feet, for the purpose of traveling or pleasure." The middle wheel was the largest, and the front and back two wheels were of equal size. The skater could roll on two wheels by bending forward or backward, or on one wheel—the middle wheel. This weird invention did make turning possible. "Hooks" in front and back of the skates worked as brakes. His skates were used in a skating exhibition on a tennis court in London. But somehow, the idea didn't catch on.

Roller skates were a novelty, not a popular sport. Several others tried to popularize it but failed. One man skated across the gardens of the Tuileries in Paris to win a bet. Others used it in theatrical acts. In the 1840s, a

In 1907 skates looked pretty much as they do today.

German beer hall employed pretty barmaids who served drinks on roller skates. Small iron wheels were used under boots, and the barmaids looked "rather weary" at the end of a night's work.

In 1849 roller skates became part of an opera staged in Paris, then London. In the third act of the opera *The Prophet,* by Meyerbeer, there was an ice skating scene. It was impossible to freeze the stage so ice skates might be used, so a machinist was called in. The machinist, a

Monsieur Legrange, produced two kinds of skates, both with iron wheels. The men performers wore skates with two wheels in a straight line under their boots. The women wore skates with four wheels, much like today's skates. (It was assumed women's ankles were weaker and needed greater support.)

The ice scene, using roller skates, amazed and delighted all who saw it. For the first time the man in the street wanted to skate. It sold well in Paris. People skated indoors on wooden and marble floors, and outdoors on the streets.

When the show went to London, the skating scene aroused great interest. During rehearsals many came to watch. Until the performers mastered their skates there were many accidents, with several young ladies of the ballet corps rolling right off the stage into the orchestra pit. It was reported that one young woman landed in the middle of a bass drum!

About the same time a ballet composer wrote a new ballet called *The Pleasures of Winter: or, the Skater.* Included in this ballet was a winter sports scene. Roller skates were disguised to look like ice skates. The stage was covered with a material which looked like ice, and music imitated the sound of gliding on ice. The audience was delighted. Roller skating looked easy because the skaters were so graceful.

Soon after, the first rinks were opened to the public, but the skates used had four iron wheels, each in a straight line from toe to heel. It's hard to imagine why the wheels weren't paired, as they are today, but perhaps the inventors were thinking of duplicating the blade of an ice skate. The poor design made it almost impossible to perform ice skating maneuvers on wheels.

In the next years many different skate designs appeared. One man patented a skate with coupled wheels in the middle and single wheels at both ends. Another changed the rollers from iron to India rubber. A skate with four pairs of coupled wheels didn't work very well

Bicycle skates, 1910.

Pedaled skates, 1910.

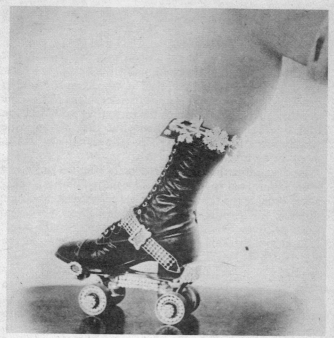

Jeweled roller skate, 1920.

either. Nor did the tricycle type—with a wheel in front and two in the back.

It wasn't until an American named James Leonard Plimpton came up with a "rocking" skate that skating took off. Plimpton, from a farming family, took up mechanics and at twenty-one had his own business building machines. Eventually he wound up in New York, took up ice skating in the winter of 1862, and loved the exercise so much he tried to figure a way to carry it on after the ice melted. He ruled out indoor ice rinks. The refrigerator hadn't even been invented yet, and ice-making know-how was more than fifty years away. He considered roller skates. But those available required enormous physical strength to turn like ice skaters could.

Plimpton played around with his own designs and in time invented and patented a skate with two parallel sets of wheels. One pair attached under the ball of the foot, and the other under the heel. The wheels were made of boxwood and worked on rubber springs. When the skater leaned to one side of his foot, the two wheels on that side came closer together while the two opposite wheels spread wider apart. This allowed the skater to move in a curved line.

And so, more than a hundred years after the unknown Dutchman fixed spools to his shoes, the Plimpton roller skate became the first workable model. At last it became possible for a roller skate to accomplish on a wooden floor or other flat surface what ice skaters could do.

To popularize his invention, Plimpton organized the New York Roller Skating Association and built a skating rink, at a cost of $100,000, in New York. He was eager to attract the "educated and refined classes" into skating. In Newport, Rhode Island, the rink association converted the dining room and patio of a mansion into a summer skating palace. Then, invitations were sent to foreign nobility, military heroes of the Civil War such as General Sherman, and big-name society and political figures. Many came, and all seemed delighted with the new sport and exercise.

One admirer wrote, "As Morse's telegraph is to commercial pursuits, so Plimpton's system of exercise is to the social and physical wants of society."

Plimpton's skate really was better than any other yet designed, and everyone rushed to imitate it. Some sixty English inventors and forty-five in other countries hurried their designs to the patent offices in hopes of bettering Plimpton's skate. But Plimpton fought the imitators in court and won. It was the Plimpton skate that would be used in rinks all over the world from then on.

A rush to build roller rinks started. All over the United States, in England, Europe, and Australia, rinks with floors of wood, asphalt, or concrete were laid down. The asphalt floors became sticky in hot weather and were soon abandoned. But concrete worked well. Then, Plimpton designed a wood floor. Narrow strips of wood, placed side by side, with the grain running at right angle to the board, turned out to be the best skating surface.

Roller rinks became so popular that in England almost every small village had a rink. In the seaside resort of Brighton, there were six! According to one writer, "London, especially fashionable London, went mad about the craze."

But there was a flaw. The roller rinks were generally quite small. A good skater had little room to try anything fancy. Figure and dance skating were discouraged by rink managers. It interfered with the round-and-round skaters, who provided the bulk of the rink income. In the late 1880s rink rules were set up to bring some order to the sport. One such rule was, for example, "Gentlemen will not soil the floor with tobacco."

The invention of the steel ball bearing gave a new interest to skating. Mass-produced skates using boxwood wheels began appearing, but the wheels didn't wear well. Hard composition and steel wheels came next, and so did books on how to skate, interest in figure skating, and rink lessons.

By 1885 America's interest in skating was high. Opening night at two new Chicago rinks saw more than 5,000 people at each place. One rink stocked 1,500 pairs of skates. Some of the city's "best people" began going to rinks, most of them sitting in private boxes and other seats to watch the people skating to live music.

Polo on roller skates, developed from the game of hockey, became popular in the 1880s. About the same time, racing on skates attracted professional skaters. In

1884 a six-day roller skating race was held at the old Madison Square Garden in New York. The winner skated 1,091 miles!

From about 1890 to 1900, people put their skates away and took up a new interest—bicycling. You could go a lot farther, and faster, too, on a bike—while sitting.

However, by 1900, skating interest renewed. Rink operators did everything they could to publicize the sport. Acrobatics on skates, comedy routines, skating on stilts, spinning, and chair and barrel jumping were all encouraged. Weddings, with the whole wedding party on skates, were arranged. One rink in Milwaukee offered $50 to any couple who would marry on skates. It was said that the king and queen of Italy practiced roller skating in the throne room of their palace!

During World War I some rinks, particularly in the war-torn countries of Europe, were converted for war industry. And afterward, though skating continued to interest many, it did not have the same enthusiastic following as before.

There were new entertainments to fill spare hours during the 1920s. Automobiles became one of the new diversions. Evenings, adults went to speakeasies, spent their time drinking and dancing the Charleston. And then, of course, there were the movies. Skating didn't die out, it just faded into the background.

Then came the 1930s and the Depression. The Depression in 1929 put many people out of work. For the next ten years, Americans had little money for frittering away on entertainment. Interest in roller skating returned because it was a cheap way to have a good time. Inexpensive skates which clamped on shoes could be bought now, and streets and roads were paved. Outdoor skating boomed with children taking over the sport. Rink skating, cheaper than most entertainment, drew its share of adults and children.

"Roller Derby," patterned after six-day bicycle races, was first held in the Chicago Coliseum in August

Roller skating teachers in Chicago, 1941.

1935. There were twenty-four teams, each with a male and female skater. Many families competed, with one team being a mother and son pair. With a prize of $1,000 offered for first place, the competition was fierce. Skaters slept on cots in the middle of the rink while the derby went on around them. An annual roller derby was held in Central Park, starting in 1933. Hundreds of amateur skaters raced along the center drive while as many as 50,000 spectators looked on.

During these years American skating developed differently from elsewhere. In England, for example, more

Skating in Central Park, New York. 1942.

attention was given to perfecting the art. Perry Rawson, a retired broker and former ice skater from New York, visited England in 1937. He was amazed at what the British were doing and returned to the U.S. with motion pictures of their advanced skills. The films captured a brother and sister team, Joan and James Lidstone, four-time British Champions. The Lidstones performed school figures, skated freestyle, and danced on roller skates. Shown in many rinks throughout the U.S., these films excited great interest among serious skaters.

Soon afterward, the Lidstones toured America to show off their fantastic skills. Not only could they do precision figures only seen on ice before, but they waltzed and tangoed as gracefully as any skateless dancer.

Challenged by the British, serious American skaters would not be outdone. Guidelines were set up by national skating organizations for figure and dance skating. Always competitive by nature, Americans were also inventive. It wasn't long before their routines were as good as, and even more daring than, anything the British could do.

Skating probably reached its greatest popularity in the 1940s. Just as almost every kid today owns a skateboard, so then, it was a pair of skates. Skates took you to the library, to school, or just around the block with other rolling friends. Rinks, too, were crowded. Servicemen brought their dates to the ballrooms where organ music boomed skating waltzes over the loudspeaker. The roar of hundreds of pairs of steel wheels on the wood floors made conversation almost impossible.

But after the boom of the '40s, it was downhill again. During the '50s and '60s, whatever respectability the sport had enjoyed was lost. This was partly due to the fact that the rinks were getting old. They were noisy, dark, and smelly, and neighborhoods had changed. People had moved out of the cities to the suburbs. The rinks were now in the older, run-down parts of town.

There were still the serious skaters traveling far to get in practice hours in the afternoons for the competitions coming up. But for the most part, rinks became hangouts for troublemakers, kids looking for a rumble or for the chance to pick up the wrong kind of girl on a Saturday night.

Roller rink fun - 1970's.

The skater's image wasn't helped by Roller Derby, either. These performers came into every American living room on the TV screen. The gum-chewing toughs gouged their fellow skater's eyes, jabbed elbows into ribs, and laughed as they chased after each other. Skating got a bad name. Parents thought twice about letting their kids go to the local rink on a Saturday afternoon.

And so, finally, into the '70s and '80s. And again, the scene shifts. All because of American ingenuity—the design of a new type wheel. The urethane wheel, adopted from the skateboard, made possible for the first time roller skating which was quiet, smooth, *and* fast. The new wheels glide almost silently on the wooden or epoxy-covered rink floors. Outdoors, they roll over cracks and pebbles like they aren't there.

The '70s saw new rinks spring up like flowers after a rain. They are more than rinks; they are entertainment centers, with rooms for disco dancing, games, and roller skating.

The newer rinks are bright, clean, inviting. At Skate-O-Rama, in Downey, California, for example, the lobby and rest area are carpeted. Green-uniformed rangers serve the food, pass out the skates, keep the floors swept. Mountains form a backdrop, with trees, sparkling with lights at night, lining the sides of the silvery floor, so like an icy pond.

Not only have the rinks changed, but the skaters, too. It's not just the kids who are skating now, but also adults. It's a family thing with mama, papa, and the five kids wheeling together on a Sunday along the boardwalks and in the parks, all across the country.

Indoors, it's still round-the-rink rolling for most people, though the music is no longer waltzes played on an organ. It's disco we hear now.

The interest in skilled skating grows. Outdoor skaters are coming indoors, not because the weather goes bad, but to learn from instructors. Competition skating, always associated with the rink, is at a high. Natalie Dunn, an American, showed the world how far America has come in figure and free-style skating. She won the world's championship three times for her country. In the summer of 1979, the American team will represent the

Today's disco skaters put on an outdoor show.

U.S. at the Pan American Games, where roller skating competitions will be on the program for the first time. And after that? The Olympics—not in 1984, but in 1988 at the latest.

Roller skating has come of age. Join the fun.

learning the
basics

EVEN IF YOU'RE as uncoordinated as a puppet, and as clumsy as a clown, there's no reason you can't skate. At the very least you should be able to learn to glide around a rink or down a street, turn, and stop. Skating backward, and more intricate movements will come later, after you've developed confidence through success.

If you can ice skate, or skateboard, roller skating will be easy. That's because you already know how to balance and coordinate your body.

But how can anyone learn skating from a book? After all, you're not about to go out on the streets all laced up in your skates—with this book in hand! Yet, it is possible to master some of the basics before ever stepping out of the house. Without skates, go through the actions described in the next pages again and again. Then, that first time you're on skates, it will be natural to take the right stance, keep the proper balance, and move correctly. All of a sudden, you'll find you can skate.

LEARNING HOW TO ROLLER SKATE IS EASY!

LET'S LOOK OVER THE SHOULDER OF AN INSTRUCTOR AS HE TEACHES SOME BEGINNERS.

FIRST, NEVER FORGET THAT SKATING IS *JUST THE REVERSE* OF WALKING! YOUR WEIGHT MUST ALWAYS BE DISTRIBUTED EVENLY OVER THE *MIDDLE* OF THE SKATE...NOT ON THE TOE OR HEEL!

HERE'S A HELPFUL EXERCISE TO LEARN CORRECT BALANCE AND POSTURE! WITH BODY ERECT, ABDOMEN AGAINST WALL, NOSE 3 INCHES AWAY, PLACE YOUR PALMS ON THE WALL AT CHIN LEVEL! THEN SHIFT YOUR WEIGHT TO THE RIGHT LEG AND LIFT THE LEFT OFF THE FLOOR...

...LIKE *THIS!* THEN DO THE EXACT OPPOSITE! THIS SIMPLE SIDE-TO-SIDE MOVEMENT IS CALLED *ROCKOVER!* REMEMBER *ALL BEAUTIFUL SKATING IS DONE FROM THE HIPS!* PRACTICE THIS AT HOME!

NOW QUICKLY SHIFT BODY WEIGHT TO LEFT FOOT, AND GLIDE FORWARD ON LEFT SKATE!

IN ORDER TO FEEL AT HOME ON SKATES.

- PRACTICE!
- GET WEIGHT OVER THE MIDDLE OF THE SKATE!
- PRACTICE MORE!
- RELAX!

KEEP REPEATING THE SIDE AND BACKWARD STROKES WITH YOUR RIGHT AND LEFT SKATES! LOOK OFF AT A *DISTANCE* WHEN YOU SKATE, NEVER DIRECTLY IN FRONT! REMEMBER *KNEE-ACTION* IS USED FOR LEVERAGE AND FLEXIBILITY!

NOW— BACK TO THE INSTRUCTOR...

LET'S GO ON TO **STROKING!** GOOD ROLLER SKATING IS SIMPLY **SWAYING STROKES** TO LEFT AND RIGHT, REPEATED OVER AND OVER!

NEVER RUN ON SKATES... LET THE SKATES GLIDE! RUNNING LIKE THIS THROWS YOU OFF BALANCE AND WILL MAKE YOU FALL! THERE'S NO NEED **EVER** TO FALL!

IN GLIDING, GRADUALLY MAKE EACH STROKE LONGER UNTIL YOU BUILD UP SPEED! KEEP GLIDING FROM LEFT SKATE TO RIGHT SKATE... SWAYING YOUR BODY REGULARLY!

OKAY, THAT'S ENOUGH FOR A STARTER! JUST REMEMBER THIS TILL NEXT TIME...WHEN SKATING, ALWAYS RELAX, BEND YOUR KNEES, USE YOUR ARMS FOR BALANCE AND SWAY YOUR BODY IN THE DIRECTION OF THE FOOT CARRYING YOUR WEIGHT!

AFTER STARTING AND STROKING ARE MASTERED THE INSTRUCTOR GOES ON...

WE'LL NOW TAKE UP *STEERING!* WHEN A SKATE TRACES A CURVE, WE CALL IT AN *"EDGE"!* IT'S ALL A MATTER OF LEANING YOUR *ENTIRE* BODY WEIGHT *EQUALLY* THE WAY YOU WANT TO TURN!

FOR LEFT TURN...*LEAN LEFT!* FOR RIGHT TURN...*LEAN RIGHT!* THE WEIGHT OF YOUR FOOT IS ON THE EDGE OF THE SKATE! DON'T SKATE YOUR FIRST EDGES TOO LONG OR TOO DEEP! ROLL *EASILY* AND IT'S A *CINCH!*

TRUE "EDGES" CAN'T BE MADE WITHOUT *SIDE LEAN!* EVER SEE A BIKE ROUND A CURVE WITHOUT TURNING THE FRONT WHEEL? THAT'S *SIDE LEAN!* SKATING LEFT OR RIGHT, YOUR BODY MUST LEAN TOWARD THE *CENTER* OF THE CURVE...!

YOU'VE *GOT* IT, JOAN! THAT'S A PERFECT EDGE-- YOUR SIDE LEAN'S JUST RIGHT!

I REMEMBERED WHAT YOU SAID ABOUT THE BICYCLE!

NOW LET ME SHOW YOU ALL THE *FOUR-WHEEL* STOP! GLIDING FORWARD ON MY LEFT SKATE, I BRING THE RIGHT SKATE UP BEHIND THE LEFT AT A 45-DEGREE ANGLE TO THE LINE OF TRAVEL!

I LET THE RIGHT SKATE *GRADUALLY* TOUCH THE FLOOR, APPLYING A *LITTLE* WEIGHT, SO THAT ALL FOUR WHEELS *REVOLVE* SLIGHTLY! *NEVER DRAG THE WHEELS!* AS I APPLY PRESSURE, I COME TO A *PERFECT STOP!*

Going into the T-stop.

What you've just learned to do is a T-stop. It's called that because the skates form a T in the process of stopping. That's the way most competitive skaters slow down or stop. But there's an easier and quicker way. Use your toe stops. Not both, but one. Drag one toe stop behind as you're skating forward on the other foot. Whatever you do, don't try to brake by standing suddenly on both toe stops. You'll be catapulted forward, like a rocket, into skaters in front.

Now that you've learned forward skating, turning, and stopping, here's the simplest form of backward skating.

1. Stand against the railing and hold on with both hands.

2. Balance over the middle of your skates.

3. Turn both toes inward, slightly. Your heels will be apart in a slight V position.

4. Bend both knees and push away from the railing with both feet. The heels will be moving out.

Finished position, T-stop.

5. When your feet are about twelve inches apart, reverse heel direction. Bring the heels *toward* each other until they are about two inches apart.

6. Your feet will be making a scissors-type movement, out and in. The heels will push out, stop, then push toward each other, then out, stop, then together. Always keep your balance in the middle of the skate.

7. Don't look down at your feet or your weight will go toward your toes.

8. Keep your body erect, with back straight. Arms should be waist high and held out for balance. Bend your knees slightly. Your head is up, and you look straight ahead. If the room is crowded, you may glance over your shoulder.

9. Both feet do the work, in and out.

For more advanced backward skating, read the following panels.

BACKWARD SKATING STARTS FROM A PARALLEL TAKEOFF, EXTENDING THE FREE OR BALANCE FOOT IN *FRONT* OF YOU--THE REVERSE OF *FORWARD* SKATING!

PLACE YOUR FEET LIKE THIS, LEFT TOE TURNED IN! NEXT EXERT PRESSURE AGAINST THE *INSIDE EDGE* OF THE LEFT FOOT, WHILE LIFTING THE RIGHT OFF THE FLOOR...

...LIKE *THIS!* I POINT MY RIGHT TOE *DOWN* AS MUCH AS POSSIBLE SLIGHTLY *AWAY* FROM MY LEFT FOOT! NOW I START SHIFTING MY WEIGHT TOWARD THE RIGHT. READY TO BRING MY LEFT FOOT TO A PARALLEL POSITION!

NOW THAT I'VE GOT MOMENTUM BY USING THIS BACKWARD PUSH AND BALANCE, HERE'S HOW WE STROKE BACKWARD! FOR BEST FORM LEAN SLIGHTLY, BEND KNEES, AND LOOK BACK OVER YOUR SHOULDER! PUSH OFF WITH YOUR RIGHT FOOT LIKE THIS AND GLIDE BACKWARD ON LEFT FOOT!

NOW BRING THE RIGHT FOOT BACKWARD AND ALONG THE LEFT! KEEP YOUR BODY ERECT--SKATING KNEE SLIGHTLY BENT!

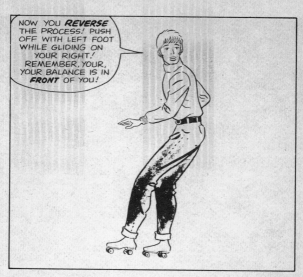

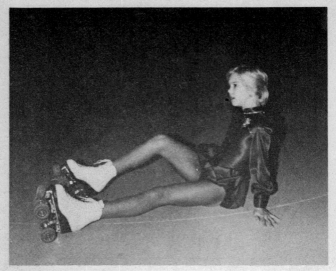

Falling properly is important.

FALLING

Everyone falls at one time or another. Don't be afraid of it. It's all in knowing how to do it.

The ground is hard and falling can mean a broken arm, a dislocated shoulder, or at least a skinned knee or elbow. If you know how to fall, you can minimize damage.

When you find yourself losing control and think you're headed for the floor, the first thing to do is relax. That may seem impossible at a time when you're most tense. But, as in any sport, bones are most likely to break when the body is stiff.

Bend your knees as you're coming down so you have less distance to fall. Don't thrust your hands out or behind you to take the brunt of the impact; you can break the wrist. Instead, try to sit down. Your bottom is better

Cross pull.

cushioned than any other part of the body. Let it take the fall. Caution: Don't lean back too far when falling. You can bruise or break your tail bone.

Now that you've learned the most basic skating movements, how about some fancy steps? Master a few tricks and you'll look like a pro.

CROSS PULLS

This is one of the easiest and most graceful moves to make. It is useful in dance and in making turns. Here's how it's done.

    1. While gliding on left foot, instead of stroking back with right foot as in regular skating, bring right foot forward. Place it over the left.

2. Gliding now on your right foot, bring left foot from behind into forward leading position again.

3. Repeat movement, with right foot crossing over left foot and gliding while left foot is raised then returned to normal position again.

Cross pulls, also called "cutting the circle" turns, lead the skater into a circular turn.

Going into a Mohawk turn.

MOHAWK TURN

   1. While skating, lift your left foot and turn it so it is heel to heel with the right foot. It takes quite a bit of stretching so don't expect to do this well the first few times.

   2. Lean in toward an imaginary circle.

   3. Hold that position if you have enough speed.

Second position. In final position, right foot is raised slightly behind and body is turned to right of photo.

4. To come out of the turn, lift left foot and bring it alongside right foot.
5. Resume skating.

SPREAD EAGLE

1. While skating, turn the left foot so it is rolling backward. Heels are spread as far apart as possible, but pointing toward each other.

Spread eagle position.

How to do 'Shoot the duck'.

2. Lean in toward an imaginary circle.

3. Hold the position if you have enough speed.

4. To come out of the turn, lift the left foot and bring it alongside the right foot. Resume skating.

Vary the spread eagle by differing arm positions. Arms may be loosely held at about shoulder level, or placed on hips, or extended opposite each other, one pointed toward the floor and one toward the ceiling. In-

vent your own variations of the spread eagle by varying
the distance between your feet, or by bending your knees
while keeping toes pointed outward.

SHOOT THE DUCK

Roll forward on both feet. Bend your knees so you're
way down. Extend one foot to the front so your weight
is in the middle of the skating foot. When ready to get

Heel-toe spin.

up, bring your extended leg back to the floor and straight up.

Care should be taken not to place weight on the heel of the skating foot and the extended foot should not be lifted too high or you may fall backward.

SPIN

The easiest spin is the heel-toe, or the two-foot, spin. The spin will be to the left.

1. Start the spin with feet shoulder-width apart, about twelve inches between them.

2. The weight is on the left foot, on the big-toe wheel, which is the inside, forward wheel. On the right foot, the weight is on the inside back wheel.

3. The left foot, as you're spinning, will be rolling backward.

4. The right foot will be rolling forward. The weight will be pressing on the inside of both skates.

5. Shoulders will rotate while the feet are rotating.

6. The head stays in the same spot. The shoulders rotate around the center which is your head and neck. You're a revolving door.

Going into the sit spin.

SIT SPIN

The sit spin combines a shoot the duck with a spin. It can also be done on four edges. The knee and hip should be in a straight line with the foot extended to the front. Arms are held over the free leg.

BEGINNING JUMP

1. Ride forward on both feet, keeping feet parallel, arms out, waist high.

2. Bend your knees and jump straight up. Come back down with the weight on the middle of the skates. Knees should still be bent to cushion the landing.

Doing figures.

Do this again and again. When you feel comfortable with the jump, try a jump with a half-turn.

Ride down the floor on both feet, bend knees, jump up. Rotate shoulders half a turn to the left. The body will end up turning in the direction of the shoulders. You'll land on both feet, facing backward. Knees will be bent on landing, with weight on the middle of the skate. You'll be rolling backward.

HOW TO DO THE FIGURE EIGHT

The figure eight consists of two circles which form an eight and are painted on the rink floor. Figure skaters are expected to trace that figure with their wheels, beginning on the right foot for the first circle, and changing to the left foot for the second. As skaters advance in ability, they must do more complex maneuvers (backward skating, for example) while their wheels draw the figure eight.

Skating the figure requires good coordination and balance. Learning how to do a figure eight is a good way to begin your competitive skating career. It is so important that at international meets only the top eight winners of compulsory figure eights may try out for freestyle finals. The overall champion is the one who gets highest combined figure and freestyle scores. Here's how to do it:

    1. Push off from a T position on the right foot from the center of the eight. Lean right into the circle. Try to complete the circle in a single stroke. The left foot will be carried in a trailing position with the toe pointing down and out. On the top of the circle, the free leg will be brought to a leading position over the line with the toe pointing down and out. The skating leg should be slightly bent, but the free leg is straight.

    2. Change feet at the center of the eight. Skating now on the left foot, the body leans left.

    3. Repeat foot change at center of the eight.

SPIRAL OR ARABESQUE

The spiral, or Arabesque, can be done either forward or backward and is easiest standing on the left foot. Rolling forward, extend the right leg to the back and lower the chest, so you're almost parallel to the floor. The head is slightly raised. The arms are held out at the waist to the side. The back is arched. The head is up. The toe of the trailing, raised foot is pointed.

THE CAMEL

Advanced skaters will want to combine the spiral, or Arabesque, with a spin. That movement is called a

The forward spiral.

camel. With the body in the spiral position, press on the inner edge of your skating foot. Your body will rotate around a stationary point.

There are four different camel edges that can be done: *an outer forward, inner back, inner forward,* and *outer back.*

To do the outer forward, roll forward on the left foot, pressing on the outside heel wheel.

To do an inner back, roll backward while spinning

with your weight on the inside toe wheel.

For the inner forward camel, roll forward on the right foot with the weight on the inside heel wheel.

In the outer back camel, the weight is on the outside toe wheel of the left foot.

Before going out on the floor, it's a good idea to do some exercises at the bar to stretch the leg muscles. Kick the leg up behind while holding onto the bar. Do this several times with each leg.

DISCO ROLLING

Probably the biggest difference between the rinks of the past and those of the present are the music and atmosphere. The skater's waltz to organ music can still be heard in many rinks, but the sound is fading. In its place is the music of the '70s. DJs command the expensive stereophonic equipment and orchestrate the intricate psychedelic lights. Rink skating at night is more than skating. It's an experience. An atmosphere of excitement and expectation floods the air. The beat is strong. It invades the body and infects the limbs. Arms and legs want to MOVE, want to respond to the rhythms. The skaters are at the mercy of the DJ. He is the Force. His choice of music turns them on and off.

But, if you have any sense of rhythm, and if you really love to dance, you can disco dance on skates just like you can without. Just let yourself respond to the music. Anything you can do at a disco dance hall is possible on skates. Better still, grab yourself a partner or bring one —and go.

BASIC DISCO STEPS

Much of disco dance skating is done on the toe stop, changing from foot to foot. However, many of the skating techniques already described can be incorporated into the dancing, also. Skating to the music, try to do jumps, cartwheels, splits, and pivot turns (turns on the toe stops).

Disco at a rink.

Hand and hip movements, of course, are as much part of disco dance as disco skating. Swaying the hips to music, touching each elbow to the extended hip, thumbing, pointing up and down—these are all movements to include on the rink floor.

A disco group at a fashion show.

SKATING WITH A PARTNER

There are two basic positions for skating with a partner, facing each other, or both facing the same direction.

Facing each other: Just as in dancing the fox trot, waltz, or any traditional social dance, partners skate so one moves forward while the other moves backward. The lady's right hand holds the man's left hand. The man's right hand is on the lady's back. Her left hand is on his right shoulder.

Facing the same direction: Both skaters are facing forward. The man is slightly behind the woman, but almost hip to hip. His right hand is around her waist. Her right

Do on skates what you'd do without.

hand may be free or the right thumb may be hooked into the man's right hand, which is at her hip. Both hold each other's left hand.

While skating together be sure to use the same foot as your partner. Both use right feet, or left feet at the same time, or there is a danger of tripping.

Dance movements can be incorporated here, such as crossing over, crossing behind, spread eagle, spirals, and forward swinging. (To forward swing, stand on the right foot while swinging the left forward, then resume stroking.) In more advanced dance skating, the man may lift the woman, but don't try this until you're very confident on skates.

58

Dance position, facing each other.

Dance position, both facing same direction, with same foot forward.

Stretching exercises.

WARM-UP EXERCISES

The first time on skates, your legs will let you know they're unhappy. They've been carrying up to five extra pounds on each foot. It's not unusual to get aches in hip and calf muscles and leg tendons.

To ease the stress on the legs, especially on cold days, it's good to warm up with certain simple exercises. Here are a few.

At the rink, before going out on the floor, take a minute or two at the rail against the wall. Hold the rail and do the following:

1. Bend right leg backward. Lift it with right hand so the heel comes as close to the thigh as possible. Repeat with left leg. This helps stretch the tendons at

the back of the calf.

2. Swing each leg from left to right, several times.

3. Holding on with both hands to the rail, bend your body and extend one leg so you are in a T position, with the leg on the floor forming the stem of the T. Repeat with other leg.

4. Raise one leg over the bar while leaning body toward that leg.

5. If you do not have a rail to hold onto, sit down on a chair or bench and raise both legs straight forward.

6. Do knee bends, while holding onto rail, or with arms outstretched for balance, if no rail is available.

These same exercises can be performed outdoors. Find any stationary object about waist level to hold onto. Also, try bending forward to touch your toes. This is great for stretching the hamstring muscles.

should you buy? when? what? and how much? ③

ROLLER SKATING IS a sport you can enjoy without ever having to buy your own skates. All you need do is go to the local roller rink, plunk down your $2.50, pick up a pair of rental skates in your size, and you've bought yourself an afternoon or evening of fun. Same for outdoors. A stop at the boardwalk rental store, a couple of dollars out of pocket, and you roll away for an hour or two of sidewalk exploring.

But—there comes a time in every *regular* skater's life when rented wheels just won't do. You want to own your own. You *need* to own your own.

There are practical reasons, of course. Your own skates would suit your specific needs best. The boots should fit better than rentals. The action can be adjusted to your needs. The wheels you choose will perform best for your kind of skating, whether it be speed, figure, freestyle, or outdoor.

And owning your own skates saves money in the long run. With outdoor rental fees running about $2.00 for the first hour, a once-a-week skater spends over $100 a year, minimum. That amount could buy a pretty nice skate. Rinks usually offer a reduction of about $.50 to skaters who own their own wheels. Why not save the $25.00 a year and apply it to a purchase?

Young rink skater.

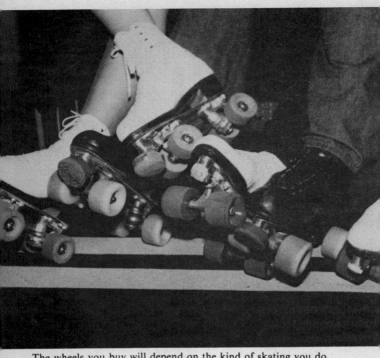

The wheels you buy will depend on the kind of skating you do.

Having your own skates available whenever you feel the urge to roll means a lot, too. Outdoor skaters, particularly, understand this. Owning your own gives you the freedom to skate *when you want,* not when the rental store is open. It frees you to skate *where you want,* not only within a half-hour's distance from the rental store.

But aside from these practical reasons to buy, there are always the emotional reasons, the gut hunger to own your own wheels. Nothing compares to holding that new skate in hand. Listen to the whisper-soft whirr of the well-tuned wheels spinning. Smell that delicious

Roller Derby skates range from a kid's first outdoor skate to competition-quality wheels.

A. The fireball, about $12.

B. Precision flyer - Roller Derby's top of the line.

new-boot scent. Run your fingers over that glove-soft leather.

Lately, every time you're at the pro shop of the rink or outdoor rental store, you linger a bit longer. The colors and shapes and varieties of choices dazzle. What would it be like to combine that boot, with that plate, and those wheels, and that toe stop, you wonder. How much would it cost? Just asking, of course.

And then . . . you're hooked.

When Should You Buy?

The rule of thumb is: Buy when skating is no longer a once-in-a-while pastime. Buy when you're skating fairly regularly, say once a week or once every two weeks and feel the interest will continue.

Buy What?

Once you've decided to own your own skates you need to ask yourself several important questions.

1. *Where will I do most of my skating? In a rink? Outdoors?*

It's important to know where you'll do most of your skating because that will influence the type of wheel and shoe you choose. Rink skating traditionally features high-laced boots and harder, narrower wheels than outdoors. The epoxy-coated rink surface is hard and slippery. The kind of wheel which rolls best on that surface would not perform as well outdoors.

Outdoors, the best wheels are wider and softer than used indoors. This permits easy rolling over cracks and bumps. The wheel is something like a blown-up balloon. Stick your finger in the balloon and it makes a dent, but take your finger away, and the balloon returns to its normal shape. That's how the softer wheels work. They *give* when they roll over a pebble or crack, then go back to their normal shape.

If you're planning to skate mostly outdoors, you'll want to consider whether high-laced boots are best, or the jogger-type shoe, or the sandal-styled "Pop

A young professional.

Wheels"; or perhaps you want to mount your own shoes or boots on skates.

For those wanting to own one pair of skates which will go indoors or out, there are answers, too. Some polyurethane wheels operate adequately in both places, though not perfectly in either. Also, skaters may buy two or more sets of wheels, a set for outside, and one for inside. Then, comes a cold, nasty day and—presto-chango!—on go the indoor wheels and off you go to the local roller disco.

> **2.** *What kind of skating interests me most? Round-the-rink or outdoor wheeling? Artistic, speed, or hock-ey?*

If you're skating at a rink and have taken a few lessons, you may decide you like skating enough to specialize. Round and round rolling, backward and forward skills are old hat. Now you see yourself doing fancy maneuvers. Maybe you want to become a freestyle skater because the grace and beauty of movement appeals to your creative instincts. Maybe you like the idea of figure skating, with its prescribed course, and ever-increasing demands for better performance. Or perhaps you're a speed skater, driven to outskate not only your best record, but everyone else's, too.

The kind of shoes, plates, and wheels chosen will differ according to the kind of skating you do. A figure skater's wheels will differ from those chosen for a speed skater; the same is true for other skate parts.

What Will It Cost?

The price, of course, matters to most people. Roller Derby makes a child's first outdoor, in-the-driveway kind of skate for a mere $6.99. For that price you get a vinyl boot with small, loose ball-bearing steel wheels. The Fireball, also made by Roller Derby, sells for about $12 and can be used indoors or out because of its urethane wheels. For a first skate, it's a deal!

In contrast, the finest pair of competition skates, with Rydell leather boots, a Snyder plate, and eight wheels at $100 per set can run to $450 or more.

For most people, the first skates they buy usually cost under $100, more in the range of $50-$90. At the $50 price, there'll be some corners cut. You may get vinyl instead of leather boots. The wheels will not be the best and may contain loose ball-bearings instead of precision bearings. Later, if the skater wants to enter competitions, the cost will go higher.

Let's say you know where you'll do most of your skating, the kind of skating you like best, and about how much you want to spend. Then what?

Each part of a skate has a particular purpose. Knowing what each can do for you will also help you decide what to buy.

THE SKATE

The skate consists of a shoe mounted on a plate which includes a truck (the steering mechanism), cushions, bearings, wheels, and a toe stop. Each serves a function.

THE SHOE

The shoe, obviously, is what you put your foot into. It should fit comfortably and not be purchased "to grow into." Parents often make the mistake of buying skates for their children that are a size or half-size too big. They figure the toe can be stuffed with cotton until the child's foot grows into it. That's unwise. Too-big shoes make the skater trip and cause blisters. Better to buy the proper size and sell it to a younger child when it's outgrown, then buy a used skate from an older child. Some rinks and skate stores put customers in touch with each other—especially during the years of fast growth.

It's the foot and ankle which tell the truck what to do. And it's the truck that does the steering. So what matters in a shoe is that it have a stiff sole and stiff enough ankle support. You're skating along and move your knee, and your foot goes up on edge. Ideally, the plate should move with your foot. If you've got a skate where there's nothing stiff or rigid at the sole or ankle, when you move your foot it's likely the foot will rotate in the shoe, while the skate goes straight ahead.

In a boot which laces up high, when you lean your ankle, it pretty much dictates that the plate has to move with the shoe and with the foot.

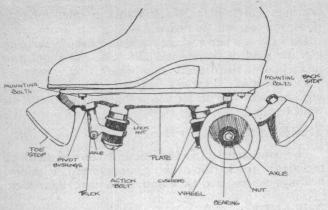

Know the parts of your skate.

That doesn't mean you must have a high-lace shoe. But you should have footwear with stiff counters and stiff soles. Test the shoe by pushing down on the sole. If it moves, don't get it.

Boots range in price from $25 a pair up to $110 for better leather, more support, and soft-padded tongues. Short shoes that lace above the ankle are fine, even for skateboard parks, but the sneaker-type shoe may not be firm enough.

Sure-Grip makes the Jogger, which is cooler, lighter weight, and more comfortable than lace-up boots. It's designed with special insole material which keeps the shoe and plate from separating. The adult jogger-turned-skater finds these skates closest to what he's used to.

Pop Wheels manufactures a sandal with wheels recessed in the wooden sole. A flip of the lever and out drop the wheels, converting the sandal to a skate. More a gimmick than a true skate, the small, close-together wheels limit turning. Still, they can be worn indoors as shoes, or skates.

Nicki Armstrong's career is really rolling along!

Almost any kind of shoe can be mounted on a skate. Cowboy boots, even ski boots.

In fact, ski skating promises to be a new and exciting sport. Just introduced by Sure-Grip, it has many assets.

Pop Wheels

Pop wheels for indoor-outdoor.

Your own ski boots can now be mounted on Sure-Grip skates and detached as easily as skis. It works much like ski bindings. A lever on the heel can be popped up or down, depending on if you want in or out. When the ski boot isn't mounted, the skate can take other boots for conventional skating.

With ski boots on skates, the body is forced into a ski stance, knees forward and weight more forward than on roller skates. By shifting weight from leg to leg as if on skis, the skater can slalom and parallel skate just as if on the slopes.

For the skier, it's a real boon. You can keep legs in shape between seasons, so that on opening day you're ready to go. You can break in new boots. Or, if you've

Sure-Grip has come out with the Roller Ski for out-of-season fun.

never skied before, you can learn on dry land with less danger of falling and breaking a leg. A few days of practice and the roller skater can move onto skis and the snow slopes with the physical savvy of the experienced.

The manufacturer expects ski resorts to pave over their bunny slopes for out-of-season roller skating. Until then, driveways and mild hills near home will provide ski skaters with practice grounds.

THE PLATE

There are three types of plates. One is *die cast*, made of aluminum alloys, generally. Die-cast plates tend to be

A die-cast plate.

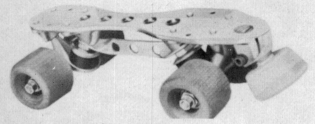

Sure-Grip's racing skate without its boot.

very lightweight and the weakest of the three types. Even though they're the weakest, they seldom break, so they're adequate for most purposes. Road Skates International has taken a die-cast plate and put a jump bar on it. A jump bar is a flat steel strip which hangs below the plate, parallel to it, and strengthens it.

Die-cast plates are the cheapest, lightest, but weakest plates, but they're strong enough, especially with the jump bar added. Chicago makes die-cast plates. So does Roller Derby.

The second plate in order of strength and price is *sand cast*. These plates tend to be heavier, stronger, and only slightly more expensive, about $2–$3 more a pair. The Sure-Grip Jogger, Super X, and Chicago 3700 plate are sand cast.

The third type is the *forged plate*. These are recognized by the flat base-plate and the jump bar. They are the strongest. Forged plates are a prestige thing. Competition skaters use them, and generally all better skaters do. The cheapest forged plates cost about $40–$50, while the die cast and sand cast cost $20–$30. Top-of-the-line forged plates, made by Snyder, are about $150.

When you buy a Chicago, Sure-Grip, or, say, a Snyder skate, what you're buying is the plate made by each of these companies. On this plate the manufacturer mounts shoes, trucks, wheels, bearings, toe stops, etc. Only Roller Derby manufactures all the parts that go into their skates.

If you're buying a skate for just round-the-rink rolling or street strolling, don't worry about what plate you buy. The skate you take home from the rink or outdoor rental shop will be already assembled. It will probably be a Roller Derby, Sure-Grip, or Chicago and cost between $49.99 and $89.99. You may want to upgrade the wheels, but otherwise you've bought and will live with the package deal.

If you're into competition skating, then the kind of plate you choose does matter. The strength of the plate, the weight of it, are considerations in speed skating as well as artistic skating, which involves jumps. While Snyder is still considered the Rolls Royce of the roller skating industry, the competition is closing in. Snyder does offer a nice incentive for buying their expensive plates. For a nominal amount, about $20, they'll take your old plate in when you've outgrown it and send you a new one. Sure-Grip offers a similar exchange arrangement, but not at all rinks.

THE TRUCK

When you buy roller skates, plates, including trucks, are included. The truck is the T-shaped metal piece which attaches to the plate at the top and holds two wheels at the bottom. Its purpose is to move back and forth so you can change direction, or steer.

With skates that use a bushed pivot (a urethane bushing, in some instances), it's possible to switch trucks

Mattel's Alpha skate (left) and Super Pro.

between skates made by different manufacturers. But, the change is hardly worth it, because truck geometries are very similar, varying mostly in material and therefore weight.

What some skaters like to do is get a whole new look by switching to skateboard trucks. For every brand skate there are several skateboard trucks that will fit. A skateboard truck is wider; it gives greater stability and looks different. There's the appeal of style, using the wider truck. But also, certain tricks can be performed more readily (the grinder, at skateboard parks, for example).

On the whole, though, stick with the truck that comes with your plate.

CUSHIONS

Most roller skates come with rubber cushions. Some

people prefer urethane. They have a much better memory. A rubber cushion on a new pair of skates changes shape too quickly. Adjust the truck, tightening down on the cushion, and go out and skate for a day. You find that the rubber has changed shape and you must readjust for it. With urethane cushions, you put them in, adjust them the way you want, and they stay that way forever.

WHEELS

Probably the most important part of the roller skate is the wheel. Go out and buy a $200 pair of skates and put on the wrong wheels, and you won't have any fun at all.

Wheels are chosen for where they will be used. A $300 pair of skates with rink wheels will be great at the rink. But take them out on the street and the wheels will be slow, noisy, they won't grip, and they'll vibrate.

In judging wheels, you go by durometer (which means degree of hardness), rebound (which means resiliency, the ability of the wheel to return to its original shape), and size. Manufacturers usually advertise their wheels as "so-and-so durometer with excellent rebound."

For the average street skater, a durometer of about 85 –88, of very high resilience, is recommended. Bones wheels are a good example, with a durometer of 90, very high resilience (which makes them fast), and very nice gripping qualities. Another good outdoor wheel is the blue Kryptonic, which is about 88 in durometer, very fast, very resilient, and very comfortable.

A lot of companies are putting out very high quality, low-priced wheels. Road Skates International in Venice, California, offers an excellent wheel for $2.50 each, for example. It's soft enough to be comfortable, resilient enough to be fast, and has very nice grip qualities. In contrast, Bones and Kryptonic cost about $6.00 a wheel.

Indoors, these wheels would be too slow because of the smoothness of the rink and the softness of the

Just a few plates and wheels on the market.

wheels. A softer wheel tends to be faster than a hard wheel *on a rough surface,* but slower than a hard wheel on a smooth surface. Indoors, a hard wheel is best.

For skateboard parks, you'll want slightly harder wheels than those used on the street because you're riding on a smooth surface. These same wheels could go indoors to the rink. Bones and Gyro wheels work well in skateboard parks and rinks. They're hard, fast, have good gripping qualities. It's most important, especially in the park, for the wheels to grip when you want them

Ask others how they like their wheels.

to, and not grip when you don't. You vary that by the force you use to push down on the wheel.

Height and width of wheels vary. Indoors, smaller wheels, both in height and width, work best when doing a lot of pivoting, spins, or speed skating.

The wider the wheel, the more friction, the more sliding, the more difficult to pivot. So, for artistic skating, indoors or out, you want a wheel to be narrower than the very wide wheels used outdoors.

The height of a wheel is important outdoors. Imagine the taller wheel. The greater its diameter, the smaller a given bump looks to that wheel. Bigger wheels tend to roll smoother and faster on rough surfaces. The most common size for outdoors is sixty-five millimeters.

Outdoor wheel companies such as Kryptonic, Powell, and Gyro, who were first into skateboard wheels, are now testing and putting out their first roller skate wheels. Widths on those will be an inch to an inch and a quarter. Wider wheels (up to three inches) give more traction, and more stability, and look neat, but they're a little more clumsy.

Wheels, too, are a matter of style. Wider wheels are used in skateboard parks, for example, probably because skateboarders use them. Narrower wheels would work just as well.

The best way to select wheels is to find out what's best for you. Go to a shop, and the salesperson usually tells you what the owner told him to say. To test the salesperson's knowledge, ask a difficult question you know the answer to. If you're not satisfied with the salesman's answer, don't trust his other advice.

The best way to find out about wheels is to talk to other skaters. Ask questions like: What kind of wheel are you using? Have you skated on any other wheels? (This last question is important because if someone likes his wheels but they're the only kind he's ever used, you don't really know if the wheels are good or not.) Ask: Do you like this wheel better than other wheels you've skated on? Why? What kind of ride does it give? Does it grip? Check ten or fifteen people and you'll begin to get a picture of which wheels skaters prefer, and why.

Trade wheels with friends. It's easy to switch wheels. It gives you a chance to try out a variety of different widths, heights, durometers, and resiliencies.

Some people own several pairs of skates. One is set up for use in the rink; one is for use in the skate park; one for street skating. But most people can't afford that. If you can only afford one pair, buy two sets of wheels— one for outdoors, one for indoors and skatepark. That's the best way to go.

One more word on the subject. There's something new going on in wheels—the aluminum core. Gyro has taken its aluminum core and, through a patented and secret system, bonded it to the urethane, which is very hard to do. What the core does is give you a rigid surface to put your bearings in. If you can imagine—when you corner on a soft wheel, the bottom of the wheel pushes in and the wheel tends to distort. The bearings have extra friction placed on them which makes you slow down on a corner. The Gyro wheel eliminates that. Your bearings stay perfectly in line, and cornering is much faster.

Kryptonics has done similar things with a nylon core, and other wheel makers are following. Speed skaters use core wheels that are custom-made for them. Core makes the wheel seem harder, so a wheel with 85 durometers containing a core will make the wheel feel like it's 88 or 90 durometers.

You measure automobile tires by how many miles they'll wear. Skate wheels, the urethane kind, should last to 3,000 miles of use. Softer wheels, being less dense, wear somewhat more quickly. Skater Clint Shaw rolled across Canada on one set of urethane wheels, the kind which sell for about $20 a set.

BALL BEARINGS

Skate wheels, regardless of type, all turn around small steel balls called bearings. There are usually eight bearings in each wheel. Loose ball bearings are found in cheaper skates. They give a good ride but tend to collect dirt and grime, so they need cleaning often.

The best wheels contain enclosed or *precision* bearings. Precision bearings are each encased in their own housing and packed with grease to protect them from contact with the dirt and grime which wear them out. They are more expensive to make. However, they give a smoother, quieter ride and may never need maintenance or replacement during the life of the skate. Until recently, it cost about $20 more for precision bearings. However, advances in design have now lowered the difference to $10. Discuss how much and what kind of skating you want with your skate-shop pro. The pro will help you decide which wheels and bearings are best for the amount you have to spend.

TOE STOPS

For both indoor and out, the best toe stops are made of rubber. Bell-shaped ones tend to work better than cylindrical ones. This is probably because they're made better.

Many people are getting into urethane and vinyl toe stops. They're prettier in color, and last longer. But when you want friction to stop, rubber is the way to go.

TOE GUARDS

A valuable addition to your skate is the toe guard. Its purpose is to protect the toe of your shoe from becoming scuffed. Beginners, particularly, tend to go up on the toe of the shoe, wearing it out. There are plastic and urethane toe guards on the market for about $3, but they're narrow, wear out quickly, and slide off the toe easily. Leather guards will be on the market soon and are recommended.

SAFETY EQUIPMENT

Safety equipment for the skateboard park is discussed in the chapter, "Skating the Skateboard Parks." Special heavy-duty equipment is recommended there. But for the general outdoor skater, especially when starting out, certain padded protection is also recommended.

No matter what your age, there's no shame in gearing up with helmet, knee and elbow guards, and wrist and palm protectors. That's true especially the first few times on skates. You may look like a Ram quarterback, but so what? It may save you from skinned elbows and knees, at the very least—broken bones or a concussion, at worst.

Most outdoor rental shops provide safety equipment and, in fact, may require its use if you're new on skates. Wear them proudly. It's "chic" to don attractive wrist guards and bright-colored elbow and knee pads. Once you're comfortable on skates you can leave them behind.

WHAT TO WEAR

Rule one for outdoor or indoor skating: Dress comfortably. Outdoors, on warm days, shorts and T-shirts, leotards, even bikinis make it—with safety equipment padding elbows and knees for the new skater.

In cold weather, the general rule is to wear clothing that isn't too tight fitting. Stretchy knit fabrics that 'give' when you reach or bend provide greater comfort than stiff fabrics.

Indoors, especially for the serious skater, women and girls generally wear leotards or short skating dresses which expose the legs. This permits skating instructors to observe leg and body movements. Also, during competition, the clinging leotard and soft-flowing skirts flatter a good figure.

Qiana is probably the most popular fabric used for skating dresses. It washes beautifully and is easy to sew. Furthermore, it doesn't fray or curl and swings freer when the skirt is left unhemmed. Qiana tends to be clingy, so the full-figured woman may want to choose another fabric. Dark colors help slenderize, so Qiana in a royal blue or dark green may hide the bulges and appear to cut off a few pounds.

Other excellent fabrics used for skating outfits, both for males and females, include Spandex, which is stretchy but a bit warm, polyester knits, acetate and other synthetic knits. Be sure the fabric has a two-way stretch, and ask if the material curls before hemming (which is a disadvantage).

Male skaters often practice in pants and a shirt at rinks. For competition, the usual costume is a one-piece, long-sleeved outfit of a stretchy fabric. Some skaters wear a body suit with pants over it. Colors range from white to—you name it.

Skating outfits may be bought at ice rink apparel shops, hosiery stores (for leotards), and recently, in some department stores. Many skaters choose to design

Comfortable clothing which gives freedom of movement is best for the skater.

and make their own outfits. Pattern books tend to be outdated for skating styles. Find a pattern maker, and once you have a standard pattern, you can vary it by choosing different colors and fabrics and by adding decals, sequins, or other decorative touches.

competition – the yellow brick road to the olympics

4

YOU MAY WELL be very happy wheeling along the streets and beach walks, outperforming the skateboard royalty in their own kingdoms—skateboard parks—or gliding to the disco beat at the local rink. And that's fine. But there are those for whom skating is more than sport, exercise, or fun. These are the 26,000 skaters from three to their mid forties registered for amateur competitive skating.

Last year, some 1,700 of them came together to test their skills in the nationals at Lincoln, Nebraska. For ten days these finalists competed for seventy-five national titles in artistic skating (figure, dance, and freestyle) and speed skating. These were the people who thought nothing of practicing six or more hours a day, every day, for years to become what they were. From them would come the recognized few who were the *very best*. And these few would represent the U.S. at the 1978 world meet in Lisbon, Portugal.

In back of each skater's mind was the knowledge that roller skating had come of age. It was the very best time to be at peak performance. From the winners at World would also come the first U.S. Pan-American roller

Students in a class.

skating team. They would represent our country in San Juan, Puerto Rico, in the summer of 1979.

And even beyond that date, the dreamers dreamed. It seemed almost certain that roller skating would finally be recognized as an Olympic sport, hopefully by 1984. The boy or girl under ten who took trophies at nationals now might well be the U.S. entry to the Summer Olympics in less than ten years. That was something to think about and work toward!

Skaters first become introduced to the idea of competing at their local roller rinks. Generally, a skater begins by taking group lessons. Class lessons run about $1.50 for a half hour, if you own your own skates; $2.00 for the same time with the rink's skates. Classes vary in size from eight or fewer to as many as fifty or more. Winter classes are the most crowded because bad weather sends people indoors.

Start with group lessons to learn balance, timing, and

Skating takes long hours of practice to be good.

coordination. If you only want to be a social skater, that's enough. If you want to get into competitive skating, you'll need to take private lessons once you've learned the basics. One twenty-minute private lesson a week is a good way to start. It will cost about $5.00 for twenty minutes. Only when learning routines as advanced skaters is it necessary to take hour-long lessons.

HOW TO CHOOSE A TEACHER

Rinks and teachers tend to specialize in a type of skating. One rink may emphasize speed skating. Another may put more attention into freestyle skating. Still another will be best at dance, or speed, or hockey.

For general overall skating, the best way to choose a teacher is to go to some of the local contests and observe. Call your closest rink and ask when the next proficiency tests are being held, and where. When you go to the test center, observe and try to decide what kind of skating you like most. Is this the kind you'd like to specialize in? If so, watch to see which skaters to that best. Find out who taught the skaters, then arrange to visit the rink during a lesson session to observe.

If you like how the lessons are conducted, then sign on with the teacher. You may have to drive a long way to get the instructor you want, but it will be worth it. Finding the best teacher for you is very important if you are serious about competitive skating.

PRACTICE

Many rinks have a club which permits students taking private lessons to skate during part of each day for a nominal fee (from about $5–$25 a month). The amount varies from rink to rink, as do the hours. A typical workout day, Monday through Saturday, might be from 2:00 P.M. to 7:00 P.M. As in all things, practice leads to progress. Eighty percent of a skater's improvement depends on regular practice, not now and then, but every day.

Students taking group lessons should skate during regular skating hours as much as possible. If you're skating often, add up how much you've spent at the rink in a month. It may be more than if you took one private lesson a week and paid the monthly rink-use fee. If so, it's time to switch to private lessons.

OLDER SKATERS

Older skaters may feel uncomfortable taking group lessons with young children. If so, join an adult class if your local rink offers one. Or, take private lessons.

THE SKATES TO USE

Once you decide to go into competitive skating, it's a good idea to buy a better skate than the all-purpose one which sells for under $70. It's easier to learn on a skate whose plate, wheels, boots, and toe stops all were chosen to fit your needs. This may be the time to invest in a Snyder plate (especially if you're very serious), the best wheels and bearings, a better boot. Figure skates will run to $450 because of the expensive wheels. Freestyle skaters may have to pay $300–$350 for the best set of wheels on a Snyder plate.

FIRST CONTESTS

When the rink instructor feels you are ready for competition, you'll be advised to buy an amateur card through the rink. For $5 you are registered for the skating year which runs from September 1 through August 31. The card certifies that you are an amateur and includes your birthdate. You must send in a photostat of your birth certificate, which is kept on file by the United States Amateur Confederation (USAC). Birthdate certification is important because all contest events are set up by age.

The first contests any skater can participate in are invitational meets. That's the name used in California. Other states may use different names. These contests are

At eight, this girl is taking trophies in Figures and Freestyle.

open to any beginners, whether class skaters (those enrolled in skating class) or otherwise. Ages range from under nine to over 35. There are three divisions: 1) Artistic Skating Union (ASU), consisting of Dance, Figure, Free Skating and Pairs; 2) Speed Skating Union (SSU), consisting of individual events and relay teams of two or four; and 3) Hockey Skating Union (HSU) consisting of Ball and Puck Hockey. As you perfect your skills, you tend to specialize. Rarely does a skater go in for freestyle *and* speed, for example, or figure skating *and* hockey.

If you're going to skate an invitational meet, you'll pay an entry fee of $2.50 for the first event and $1.00 for each additional event you enter.

FREESTYLE

For freestyle contests, you'll be expected to perform a routine to music in about two minutes, depending on age group. The older skaters skate longer—four minutes for girls, five for boys. The routines vary with each individual's ability. Your teacher helps you program the routine. The teacher should know what you do best and will choreograph, that is, map out a routine to show you off and minimize your weaker abilities. You'll do jumps, spins, and footwork. Footwork is a blending of steps between the jumps and spins. It includes turns, spirals, and arm positions which blend in with music. The teacher generally chooses the music to go with your routine.

At its best, freestyle skating is breathtakingly beautiful. The skates seem part of the skater as he or she glides, spins, and jumps—arms, even fingers, are responding to the music. It's a bird soaring, dipping, gliding on a cloudless sunny day. To be able to make it look easy, though you're wearing up to five pounds on each foot, takes skill, persistence, endurance, top physical health, and talent.

Natalie Dunn won the World championship three times for women's Freestyle.

Linda Todd and Charles Kirchner, Junior International Dance champs.

DANCE

By the time you enter dance competitions, you'll have learned how to skate to waltz, tango, and foxtrot music. More advanced skaters can disco dance and jitterbug, but these skating routines are not part of the USAC competitions. Disco-type movements can be part of a competitive routine, however.

Judging is based on performance of certain movements done to music. Just what movements you'll be required to do will be explained and taught to you by your instructor long before the contest. Each skater competing will be expected to do the same movements to the same music in the same place on the floor.

International dance competition incorporates a free dance routine for those who have qualified during compulsory dance. The scores are added together to determine the winner.

FIGURE SKATING

All contests for figure skating are based on skating along a prescribed figure eight drawn on the floor. For each contest, the skater must perform a given set of movements. The variety of skating steps done on the figure eight goes into the hundreds. For beginners, the skater does simple maneuvers.

Figures are judged on how well the skater stays on the line, on body position, take off, on the placement of turns, and on stopping. In high divisions (juniors, seniors, for example), the requirements become much more demanding. An elementary division skater may be required to skate the figure eight on one foot, forward or backward. A senior division skater would be expected to complete the figure using a variety of turns. There are twenty-two figure eights the senior skater must know and perform well.

SPEED SKATING

About a third of all registered competitive skaters are speed skaters. They include girls, as well as boys, although boys tend to dominate this kind of skating. Racers are judged on doing sixteen laps in as little time as possible. Competitors are grouped by age.

If this kind of skating interests you, choose a rink which specializes in speed skating, if possible. Rinks in

Twelve-year-old Trisha Hiller won both speed and artistic events at National competition in 1978, for elementary girls.

Speed skaters at competition. Chris Synder is behind.

1978 Senior Ladies Champion Linda Dorso skated 500 m. in 58.5 seconds, a new record.

large cities often specialize—some in roller hockey, others in speed skating, others in artistic skating. At a specialized rink, you find the teachers and the skaters with your interests to spur your competitive instincts. The rink would have information on when and where competitions are held.

Speed skating is emphasized more in Europe than in the U.S. There, the tracks are often banked, and outdoors. Americans have never performed as well as foreign speed skaters because they have had no outdoor tracks on which to practice.

In 1978, for the first time, the American Speed Team showed what it could do. Ten years before, our skaters did poorly in world speed competition in the distance races. But in 1978, three weeks of training on outdoor tracks before the meet made a difference.

The 1978 World Speed Competition was held in Mar del Plata, Argentina. Both the American men's and women's teams put in daily practice on a 100-meter banked track, whenever weather permitted. By the end of that time, handling the banked tracks was no problem. But endurance on long straightaways was.

The American men—Chris Snyder, Ken Hutter, Ken Sutton, and Pete Skias—were excellent on cornering, running low in the bank, passing skaters, and then holding position into the straightaway. But the Italian teamwork was better.

In the last race, the men's 10,000 meter final, the Italian team tried to control the race from the very beginning. The pace was relentless all through the race. Chris Snyder and Ken Hutter stayed at the back of the eighteen-man final. Just in front of them were three New Zealand skaters. When they moved to the front, with eight laps still to go, Chris and Ken went with them. On the last lap, with fans cheering them on, Ken and Chris made a low pass on the bank, then sprinted for the finish line. They came in third and fourth. Watch out world for the American Men's Speed team in the PanAm games.

The women's team—Marcia Yager, Robin Wilcox, Karen Johnson, and Gayle Falconer—were fine on a one-lap basis. But where endurance counted, they fell short. Gayle made eighth place in three races. Lack of experience in outdoor skating was the problem for both men's and women's teams.

To train for the meet, Chris Snyder, twenty-two, and skating since he was three, had gotten up at 4:30 each morning for over a year. He speedskated the quiet Dallas streets to his job at the Ft. Worth Airport—some

Roller hockey player.

seven and a half miles from home. During the workday he put in an hour or so of weight training. Then he skated the seven and a half miles back home. That's the kind of determination and effort needed in this sport.

The earliest speed contests (under age eight) are, of course, much less demanding than a world meet. Instead of racing 10,000 meters, the young racer is clocked on 200-, 300-, and 400-meter distances. As the speed skater gets older, the distance tested increases.

Two- and four-man teams compete in some contests in relay speed races. A typical senior mixed relay (both males and females on the team) requires each team member to skate 500 meters twice in a 4,000 meter race.

ROLLER HOCKEY

The hockey skating union (HSU), one of the three divisions of USAC, includes Ball Hockey and Puck Hockey. Ball Hockey is the official roller hockey game. It is this game which is played for international and world competition under the direction of the International Federation de Roller Skating (F.I.R.S.).

Puck hockey permits the use of standard hockey sticks and a collapsible plastic puck. Puck competition, however, is limited to games, tournaments and championships not higher than national level. This division isn't recognized for international competition.

Hockey is a team sport which is why a skater must be a member of an HSU club to participate in competition. A hockey club must have at least five applicants before it can be officially registered by USAC.

Last year, the eight-member U.S. team competed at a world meet in San Juan, Argentina. There, hockey is a fever, an epidemic. Five of the American team, from Pennsylvania, had rolled their way to victory in the Senior Gold Division in the 1978 National Ball Hockey Championships. The other three earned their way to San Juan through outstanding performances in National competition.

The U.S. team finished fifth out of 12 competing teams, behind Argentina, Spain, Portugal and Germany. In the years Americans have been competing internationally in hockey, the sport has received little support. In contrast, European teams play together all the time and are sponsored by their governments.

If your interest is to become active in roller hockey, first become a first-rate skater. Check the rinks in your city. Try to find one with a teacher who specializes in this sport, and where there is a team you may become part of.

AFTER INVITATIONAL MEETS

Invitational meets (or the equivalent in states other

Roller hockey game.

than California) are held many times during a given year
in each state. This gives skaters perhaps six or eight op-
portunities to compete.

Generally after you have won a certain division two
times (speed skating is considered a division, for example), then you are considered too advanced to compete
again. It's time to move on to the next stage—the more
advanced *regional* championships.

REGIONALS

Each state is part of a region. Each region incorporates several states. Not only do skaters compete
by region, but also by age. The age groups are limited,
to about two years. That means a ten-year-old will be

competing only with skaters within two years of that age, not with fifteen-year-olds.

The level of performance varies greatly. Some skaters have just come out of junior olympic competition. They were tops there but will now be competing with skaters just as good and much better. Some of the competitors are already national champions.

To win trophies, the skater needs to constantly improve. Choreography must become more original and demanding. Dance routines and figures require more exacting, difficult skating. Speed and distance skated goes up with age.

Winners take trophies—sometimes a victory symbol, or a skate or skater on a stand. In speed contests the

Senior dance champions John LaBriola and Debra Coyne.

winners gets points. At the end of the year the trophy is given according to the number of points won.

NATIONALS

Once a year skaters gather to qualify for national competition. To go on to nationals, they must earn first, second, or third place in the division they choose, within their region.

The United States is divided into eight roller skating regions. Each region may include a number of states close to each other. All skaters who compete at the national level have already taken trophies at their state and regional championships, so the competition level is now very high.

Nationals are held each summer during late July or early August. There are forty-nine categories of competition in artistic skating, and twenty-six in speed skating. Skaters from preschool age through adult compete in freestyle, figure and dance, and solo and relay speed skating. Hockey competitions are held separately at other times during the year.

To take a trophy at nationals puts you into a very elite and small class of skaters. Some 1,700 compete, but only 147 take artistic trophies and seventy-eight receive awards for speed skating.

There is a special division for artistic skaters called Senior International Division (men and women). In the freestyle category, skaters must first qualify for finals by skating figures. If they rate as one of the top eight in their figures, they go on to skate freestyle. The points from figures and freestyle are then added together to determine the overall champion.

In International Dance, the skaters must first qualify for finals by skating compulsory dances. When they make finals in their dance, they go on to skate free dance. The points are added together just as in freestyle to determine overall champion.

There's another division for mixed pairs. Here the

man and woman perform lifts and spins together.

First, second, and third place winners in the international divisions go on to the world meet, also held annually. Speed skaters chosen to represent the U.S. in the world meet must also be junior or senior men or women taking first through third place.

PAN AMERICAN GAMES

The two highest placements from each country in each category at the world meet qualify to perform at the Pan American Games.

PROFICIENCY TESTS

If you don't want to get into competitive skating, there is another kind of skating possible. The RSROA has a program of proficiency tests to determine the skill level of each skater. You are not competing with others, but rather with yourself. There are requirements for different levels of proficiency. As you pass each test, you receive a bronze, silver, or gold bar.

Proficiency tests are set up through skating centers belonging to RSROA. You learn of the dates and what you need to perform by attending classes, either group or private. Anyone may take these tests.

ADVANTAGES AND DISADVANTAGES OF COMPETITION

Competition is not for everyone. For one thing, it requires many hours of time, usually after school and often on weekends. Not everyone is willing to devote so much effort and time in the hope of reaching the top. It takes not only the efforts of the skater, but often the cooperation and support of the entire family. The skater may only be able to use the rink during dinner hours. The hours dedicated to practice, plus the need to keep up schoolwork leaves little time left for part-time jobs or help around the house.

Lavish costumes and production numbers are typical of the Gold Skate Classics.

And the competitive skater needs financial help. Skates, skating costumes, lessons, and travel to and from competitions mount up.

Still—there are many important advantages to competing. The discipline of learning to do something well spills over into other aspects of living. Self-confidence develops. The champion skater is almost always a poised and good student.

Finally, the really best skaters may find themselves headed into rewarding careers. No longer need they quit

XII GOLD SKATE CLASSIC

skating, or go to it part time when they reach twenty. Today, skating teachers are in great demand, and jobs for the best skaters exist in the entertainment industry.

GOLD SKATE CLASSIC

Every February, it's show-time, fun-time, far-out-time in Bakersfield, California. That's the time for the Gold Skate Classic. The skaters begin arriving by car, bus, and plane from other parts of California a day or two before the event. Many have been regional or national champions in dance and freestyle roller skating. They bring with them extra wheels, extra skates, suitcases full of stunning costumes, and records or tapes of the music to be played for their routines.

Often, the advanced skaters who belong to the same rink travel together. They have worked out group routines and planned their music around a special theme. Maybe they'll dance-skate to the music of *West Side Story,* dressed in the fashion of the street-wise gangs of the '50s, acting out the roles of the famous musical. Or perhaps they'll put on a production based on a South Sea island theme; the skaters will portray everything from sea captains to pineapples, from Indian princesses to orchids, native drummers, to wind maidens.

Tension runs high toward the end of the second day when winners are announced. Categories of competition are broad enough to include almost anyone. There are prizes for singles, pairs, and groups, according to age. Judges are looking for exceptional performance, interpretation of theme, how music and costume contribute.

The final event of the weekend is group production numbers. Sometimes, as many as a hundred skaters are on the floor together. Colored spotlights follow the extravagantly costumed skaters as they interpret the music and theme. For a while, Bakersfield's arena becomes a brilliant stage with the vitality and excitement of Mardi Gras.

117

Last year, some of the youngest performers on the Gold Skate Classic were invited to appear on Jerry Lewis's muscular dystrophy telethon. Roller skaters have been very active in raising funds for the disease. In 1978, $2.5 million were contributed through rink fund-raising events.

Motion picture producers will be attending the 1979 Gold Skate. They will be looking for exciting production numbers and seeking individual skating talent to appear in future films.

ROLLIN' '79

The East coast's answer to the Gold Skate Classic is an annual skating event held in Edgewood, Maryland. Its name varies from year to year, but the Las Vegas-style show has been held each year in April since 1970. Outstanding competitive skaters are invited to audition for individual or production number parts. As in the Gold Skate, the lavish costuming, staging, music and choreography make the show exciting entertainment. Thousands attend the extravaganza and proceeds go to support medical research and youth activities.

skating the skateboard parks

THE MARINA DEL REY SKATE PARK in southern California is one of the newest in the country, and one of the best. It's a Saturday morning in February. Sweater weather, with a clear blue sky and a slight breeze. Kids on skates or with skateboards under their arms or feet are heading up the steep ramp to the admission building.

Inside, every pinball machine is working, pinging out individual melodies, and a small crowd clusters around the corner to sign in and maybe rent equipment before rolling out to the outdoor park beyond.

Marina Park charges an annual membership fee of about $5. (Fees vary from park to park.) The cost covers admission, but not use of the runs. You have to sign two forms. One waives the park's liability in the event of an accident. The other instructs the park what to do for you in an emergency. The I.D. card you receive carries your picture. Every time you visit the park it's $3 for two hours' use of the runs.

What makes Marina Park one of the best is the progresssion of runs. A beginning skater can go there and find places to skate which are challenging and safe. The advanced skater can also find challenge. There are five different bowls, modeled after swimming pools. The easiest run is the freestyle. This area has a large, flat bottom and some very mellow, banked sides.

The purpose of the freestyle area is for beginning

When your wheels touch the tile, you *hear*, *feel* and *see* you're at the top.

skaters and for freestyle-type roller skaters and skateboarders. The freestyle skater tends to do very fancy maneuvers on the flat ground and banks, similar to what can be done in a rink. The banks make it possible to roll from the level up a bank, do a pirouette by rising up on the toe of one foot and do a 360-degree turn on the front wheels.

Aerial maneuvers can also be done in the freestyle bowl and often are—in competitions. An aerial maneuver is when the skater lifts both wheels off the ground. It differs from a jump in that the sloped terrain is used as the lift. The skater rolls up a bank and uses the bank to propel him up in the air rather than going up completely on leg power as in a flat rink.

The hardest bowl at the Marina Park is eleven feet deep with about four feet of vertical. The ideal bowl is ten to twelve feet deep, with two to four feet of vertical terrain and tile and coping.

The tile is the different colored tile around the top of the bowl. It acts as a signal. As your wheels roll over the gaps in the tile, you *hear* clicking noises, *feel* the difference on your skates, and *see* that you're near the top because the tile is a different color. So the tile has a purpose, to tell you when you're at the top of the bowl.

The coping is the lip that protrudes into the bowl directly over the tile. Its purpose is to give the final signal. It tells when you're leaving the bowl. You feel it as a bump when your wheels run over it.

The coping is also used in various tricks the skater might do, for example, the *grinder*. To do this, the skater places his wheels on either side of the coping and actually grinds his truck as he skates along it.

Another trick is a stall, or lock-up. A skater goes up the wall and ends up placing his feet on the coping so the coping is between the front and back wheels. Two variations of this trick are the front-side and back-side lock-up. The harder of the two is the back-side lock-up. In this, the skater is facing out of the bowl. To come out of a backside lock-up, take your lead foot off the coping and start it coming down the wall. As you begin going down the wall, turn your back foot around so the toe is pointing out of the bowl. The heel will be pointing into the bowl as you continue in the side surf position down the wall.

For the front side lock-up, the skater is facing out of the bowl. To come out of the lockup, pick up the forward foot and turn it around backwards, which puts you into a side-surf position. Then, side surf back into the bowl.

Another run to be found in skateboard parks is the slalom. Generally, it's set up with a long, flat incline with the sides bounded by banks. When used as a standard downhill slalom, cones are placed on the flat part of the run and the rider goes between them. Or, the slalom can be used as a bank slalom. Cones are placed on the banks and the rider goes between, much as a skateboard slalom.

There are many other type runs, such as half-pipes, which are circular half-sections—a long pipe with the top cut off. And even full pipes. In the full pipe, maybe twenty feet in diameter, the object is for the skater to go past vertical, past the halfway-up point. A full loop is almost impossible. A long ramp is needed to get into the pipe at full speed, or you're likely to drop from the top.

STARTING OUT

Before going into a skateboard park, you should be very comfortable on your skates. You shouldn't have to think where to put your feet. You should know instantly which way to move your foot when you're off balance. You should know how to stop *very well*.

The skates should be part of your body before you even consider trying the skateboard park. It's a good idea to visit the park first, before bringing your skates—just to look the place over.

It's the first time. You glide out into the park and

The grinder.

Side-surf position.

look around. Good hard rock is blasting out of the loudspeaker, creating an energy that makes you want to get going. Skaters and skateboarders are lined up at the entrance to every bowl. In the nearer runs, you catch glimpses of bodies rising up to the lip, then rushing back down. At the more advanced bowl, someone on skates has flipped over and then disappeared. Wow! That's for you. How do you start?

At the top, flipping and going down into a backside carve.

Slowly.

The very first time you visit a skateboard park, make a firm promise to yourself. Promise you'll only do what you feel comfortable doing, regardless of how easy it looks. Good skaters make it look easy, but don't be fooled. It isn't.

What's more, it's dangerous. You can break bones in a skateboard park. You can get a concussion, or fall on your face and grind your nose. Skateboard park roller skating deserves special respect. Go slow. Do less, rather than more.

Start in the freestyle area. Plan to spend a week there,

at least three visits, anyway. It's the easiest part of the park. You want to become comfortable with the banks there, first.

If you can side-surf, or spread eagle (see chapter 2 on how to), you're ahead. In fact, you should know how to do this before going to the park. Spread eagle should be

learned on flat ground. It takes about two weeks to learn to go heel-to-heel in a straight line comfortably. Start by pointing your feet in opposite directions and trying to describe a circle that way. Find the largest circle you can do with good form, and with each day, enlarge that circle. Eventually, you will be traveling heel-to-heel in a

An aerial.

Coming down.

straight line. It's well worth the effort to master the side surf. It's far safer to "skate" parks this way than in the feet parallel position!

When you've mastered the spread eagle in a straight line, you're ready to go into the first bowl—the freestyle area.

If you're brave enough to start at the top of the run, pick the most gradual slope into the freestyle area. Before taking off, think ahead. Pick a line you're going to travel. Go down the most gradual bank and there will be an opposing bank to ride up. Do some kind of turn on the opposing bank and return.

Set yourself a realistic limit. The first time in the park, for example, it's not important to reach the top of the wall. The advanced skaters will be flying over the walls. Don't be tempted. You're a beginner. Choose a line to go maybe halfway up the wall.

What you'll try to do is skate a backside carve. A carve is a maneuver where you describe a smooth line in the bowl, or on the bank. When you reach the top point, you are looking down into the run and your back side is facing out of the run. Reverse, and head up the opposing bank, again with your back side facing out of the run and your body looking down into the run when at the top point.

A carve takes speed. A beginning skater sometimes gets to the top of the carve and stalls. When this happens, do a kick turn. Pick up the lead foot, lift it off the ground and replace it so it's closer to the bottom of the bank, facing towards the bottom of the bank. While picking up the lead foot, pivot on the toe of the back foot until it's pointing on a line that goes down the hill. Proceed down the bank.

Variations of the carve include going up, pivoting on one foot, and coming straight back down. Aerials— where you go up, leave the bowl, and come back down —are also variations but not considered a true carve. In a carve you follow one, smooth, flowing line.

When you go to a new park, a place you've never skated before, look the run over carefully before deciding if you'll enter it. If it looks a bit too steep, walk backward down the chute, halfway, on your toes. Hold yourself steady for a moment on the toes. You are now facing the direction you entered. Then, turn one foot perpendicular to the other so it acts as a brake. You're now looking down into the run. You're on a grade. You're holding in a T-stop position. Now, pick up the back foot and turn it around and start going. Choose a low line about halfway up the wall to roll up.

Remember: Banks are something you're not used to at all. They are much steeper in a skateboard park than anything you ever skated on the streets. Be cautious.

MORE ADVANCED

When you've mastered the freestyle area—skated to the tops of its banks many times with confidence— you're ready to try something harder.

Choose the next most difficult bowl. But again, take it easy. Don't try for the top of the bowl at first. Possibly start your run halfway down the chute.

SKATING MANEUVERS

There's little value in explaining how to do a particular trick in a book. More important is being familiar with your skates, and using caution.

The best way to advance your technique is to watch other skaters. What's so neat about this sport is that everyone loves to help. People enjoy teaching each other. Skateboard parks, as well as all outdoor skating places, are community schools.

Don't be ashamed or afraid to ask for help. If you fall, don't be embarrassed. Everyone does. When you want to learn how to do something, watch the person who does it well. Then, just approach that person and ask, "How do you do that? Can you show me?" After a while, when you've become experienced, the beginners will be asking you the same questions.

If you skate often enough, the skates become part of your feet. You learn by doing. It's much like dancing. You invent a new way by combining known moves into new combinations.

SPECIAL EQUIPMENT

No other place demands good safety equipment as much as the skateboard park. In parks, you can fall from the top to the bottom of the bowl, ten to twelve feet. You MUST protect your head, elbows, wrists, hands, and knees. Anyone who is just learning is going to fall; you're doing things you're not familiar with, so it's natural.

Elbow and Knee, Hand and Wrist Protection.

When wearing good pads, you learn to fall without fear of being hurt. You fall where the pads are—on your knees, your elbow, your hands. If you're not wearing equipment, you fall on your hands, and at the very least, they'll sting. At worst, you'll break the wrist. If the elbow or knee is unprotected, think of the skin you'll burn or lose.

In street skating, the minimum padding is fine—the kind used by basketball players on knees and elbows. You're not likely to fall far, or as hard, so the most common street injuries—bruises and scrapes—can be avoided with minimal padding.

But for park skating, heavy-duty safety equipment is needed. Most people prefer the knee and elbow pads with the hard plastic caps over them, like those made by Norcon, Condor and SanJohn. The cap fills two purposes. First, it spreads impact evenly. Second, it has a low-friction sliding surface. When you fall, *it stays on your knee and slides.* Leather pads, in contrast, grip the concrete which makes impact harder. So, choose a pad with some padding in it, but most important, with a hard, plastic disc on the outside.

Wrist guards are important because most have some

Safety equipment.

kind of palm protector. They also eliminate a common
injury, which is the sprained and broken wrist. When
you fall backward, you tend to twist your wrist backward to cushion the jolt. Wrist guards give a little extra
stiffness and support. Some guards are quite attractive,
too. This would seem unimportant, but skating is very
fashion oriented. A woman, particularly, likes to wear
an attractive wrist guard. Wrist braces with palm pads

Safety equipment for street skaters.

made by Hobie, SanJohn and Condor are particularly recommended.

Head Protection

Unless you're the kind who falls head first, helmets aren't really necessary for street skating. But in the

Riding the tiles.

skateboard park, helmets are absolutely essential because head injuries are common.

Many helmets used in skateboard parks are adapted from ice hockey. Much of the other protective equipment is also.

Good brands of helmets tend to be a little heavier and warmer than the wearer likes. Protek makes a good helmet, and so does Cooper (which specializes in hockey equipment). Both offer good protection but some are a bit heavy and hot.

There are some lightweight helmets that are more comfortable but don't offer quite as good protection. Cooper makes a lower priced helmet, the SK-300, of this kind. Norcon makes some lightweight helmets that are comfortable and offer pretty good protection. A lot of skaters wear these kinds and get adequate protection. A helmet made by Kenoa Surf, called the J. Adams Flyaway, is of lightweight fiberglass. It emphasizes style and comfort a little to the disadvantage of protection but works pretty well. Most helmets made today give adequate protection, but remember—the heavier, the better.

Skaters who ride the bowls in skateboard parks are a special breed. Surprisingly, they're usually not converted skateboarders. They're skilled roller skaters with a sense of danger. You'll find them on weekends practicing their skills for six hours at a time, and when they're through at the park, it's off to the streets with them.

Park skating isn't for everyone. The difficult acrobatics, the danger put many off. Yet, for those who love it, there's nothing to match the thrill of rolling into the deep ravine, and climbing its steep walls to poise for a second at the rim. Then, for an instant free, the skater does a double turn and lands once more on the vertical wall, headed down and down, and up again.

outdoors – fun and games

RIDDLE: WHAT DO Central Park in New York, the streets of Minneapolis, and the boardwalk at Newport Beach, California, have in common?

Answer: Roller skating.

Roller skating's taken to the outdoors again. It's been outdoors before, but never as it is now. Before, in the '40s and '50s, especially, it was for the kids. Now, skating belongs to all ages.

Mothers push their babies, go to the supermarket on skates. Kids slalom down hills—on skates. Families, from grandpa down to little Joey, age four, roll along the park paths and boardwalks on weekends. It's not unusual to see pizza being delivered by a skating delivery person.

It's an eight-wheel drive world.

The skate capital of the country is probably where the big outdoor boom started—in Venice, California. There, an enterprising young man named Jeff Rosenberg opened a small roller rental shop about three years ago and called it "Cheapskates."

Soon after, two friends, Suzanne Thomas and Phil Lacy, quit their jobs at a mental hospital and pooled their funds. They bought thirty pairs of roller skates and rented them from a VW van set up near the beach.

On course.

Thomas and Lacy formed Road Skates International when they got the idea of using skateboard wheels on standard skates. Chicago Skate Company backed them, and now they're doing a brisk business selling their skates in the United States, Japan, Europe, and Canada

Skate rental in California.

—all from a start in a van. Rosenberg's Cheapskates, meanwhile, is very big business, supplying skates all over the country.

A typical sunny weekend in Southern California sees skaters lined up at one of the many rental shops along

Outdoor skating to a disco beat (note the earphones).

142

the beaches. They're waiting their turn to rent wheels.

Meanwhile, the action is on the beachwalk. There the joggers pass the walkers, and the bicyclists compete with the roller skaters. There are rules of the road, and most people obey them.

Along the side streets of the beach towns are the barrel-jumping skaters, the acrobats who leap over two, three bodies, the skating hockey players who use pop cans for pucks, the slalom skaters skimming around beer bottles and garbage cans.

It's glorious. Free. The way life should be. The sun warms the face. Gulls swoop and shriek overhead. Fish-smelling sea air and hot-dog scents mix deliciously. It's so GOOD to be alive and rolling along. On one side— the beach, the sandpipers picking their way delicately along the shore. On the other side—the street life: rock musicians practicing their routines; people strolling through the open-air fairs, checking the bargains in used jeans and wild T-shirts.

Not every city has its Venice, California, or Central Park, but every town and every city offers lots of places to skate outdoors.

. . . Skate along the streets of your neighborhood with all your senses engaged. Smell, feel, listen. The new wheels are almost silent, so bird calls, music, the rustle of leaves become part of the experience.

. . . School playgrounds on weekends or after school are perfect places for group games and for learning new skating maneuvers.

. . . Parking lots make great outdoor rinks, after business hours or on weekends or holidays, when empty of cars. (Some owners may deny use because they could be sued if you hurt yourself on their grounds.)

. . . City parks with their paths and bikeways are perfect for skaters. Some parks close their roads to cars on Sundays (Central Park in New York and Golden Gate Park in San Francisco, for example), leaving safe ribbons of concrete for skaters.

Jumping barrels.

The train.

   . . . Check the rules in your city for use of bike paths. Are skaters allowed, too?

   . . . Use your driveway for a slalom course, but make sure you can see ahead to the road. Skate in the empty two-car garage. Skate an empty swimming pool, but get permission first.

RULES OF THE ROAD

Observe the same courtesy rules you would if you were on a bike or driving a car. Traffic on streets and bike paths usually move in two directions, going and coming. Don't try to go against the traffic flow. If you want to pass a pedestrian or cyclist, call out the direction you intend to pass. Say, "Passing on the right," or, "Coming by on the left."

Slalom course.

GAMES TO PLAY ON SKATES

There is no end to the variety of games you can play on skates. About anything you can do on two feet should be even more fun on skates.

- Basketball on skates? Why not?
- Soccer
- Baseball
- Frisbee
- Touch-tag . . . handball . . . street hockey. All these activities become new and more exciting when played on skates.

Set up an obstacle course using books, bricks, cans, and play follow-the-leader. Time each player to see who makes it through the course fastest without knocking down any of the obstacles.

Set a course of several miles, and starting together, see who skates it fastest.

On Halloween go out in costume on skates. Hold a party in which the scavenger hunt must be conducted on skates.

Offer to teach younger children tricks you've learned, once you become a good skater. You could charge by the hour.

In terms of health, roller skating ranks third as the best physical activity to keep in shape. And it's fun. Someone who can't run a mile *can* skate five or six miles with less strain.

DIET

In any sport, it's important to eat properly and get enough rest to do your best. Same is true for roller skating. Give the body a good balance of protein, fruits, vegetables, and grains, and it will perform at its best. Skaters should allow themselves adequate rest, approximately eight hours a day. Smoking isn't advised because it reduces lung efficiency.

Shoot the duck.

The five-barrel jump.

EXERCISE

Certain exercises help build the muscles most used in skating. Unlike running, or even ice skating, roller skating requires carrying extra weight on each leg, up to seven pounds, depending on the size of the skate and materials. Hip and leg muscles need building so the extra weight will be effortless. Warm-up exercises, described in the chapter on how to skate, done regularly, accomplish this kind of muscle building.

For dance skaters, those who will be lifting or swinging a partner, shoulder muscles need strengthening. A program of weight lifting and push-ups helps develop these muscles. Swimming is another excellent exercise for shoulder, hip, and leg strengthening.

caring for your skates

TREAT YOUR SKATES kindly. Take care of them, and they'll last longer, skate better, and need much less maintenance. Here are some general rules. Follow them, and those beautiful new skates will perform as well for you next year as they do today.

1. Inspect your skates before each use. Are all nuts tight? Toe stops secure? Do wheels roll freely? Loose-ball wheels should have a little sideways shake to allow free movement of the bearings.

2. Adjust your skates for your weight and skill. Truck action should be free enough to respond easily to your body motion. Don't make the action so loose that the wheels can touch the skate plate, though. Be sure the action nut is retightened against the skate plate after adjusting.

3. Maintain your skates. Loose-ball wheels should be oiled once or twice a month. One drop of oil in each side of a wheel is enough. Don't overoil or the bearings will attract extra dust. Check rubber inserts and action cushions for wear and replace when needed. Examine ball bearings and cone nuts for wear. Keep boots polished.

Most skaters can easily maintain their own skates. The mechanism is fairly simple. The wrenches for undo-

Inspect your skates before each use.

ing parts usually come with the new skate or can be bought at the skate supply shop. Solvents, greases, polishes are all common materials found in hardware stores.

SHOES

Perspiration produces salts which leak into leather and cause it to become brittle. There are many leather conditioners on the market. Use them both inside and out to keep the leather soft and neutralize the salts. If the inside of the boot begins to smell unpleasant, use a spray deodorizer meant to refresh shoes.

BEARINGS

The best way to avoid having to clean the wheel bearings is to keep them from getting dirty. That means tak-

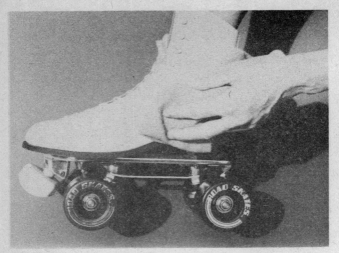
Polish the boots regularly.

ing precautions when skating, particularly outdoors. Don't go through mud, sand, water, or dirt. They're deadly for bearings.

Loose ball bearings gum up faster than the sealed, precision ones. But even the precision bearings may need cleaning sometime during the life of the skate.

How do you know if the bearings need cleaning? Spin each wheel separately and listen. Is the sound steady? Does the wheel turn evenly? Or, can you feel a small hesitation and hear a tic-tic sound as the wheel spins? If so, the bearings need cleaning.

You have a choice. Give the job to a pro at the skate shop. For about $5, he'll clean and repack the precision bearings of all eight wheels and have the skate back to you within a few days. Or, you can do the job yourself. Here's how:

1. Remove the nut locking the wheel onto the axle.
2. Pop the bearings out of the wheel. To do this,

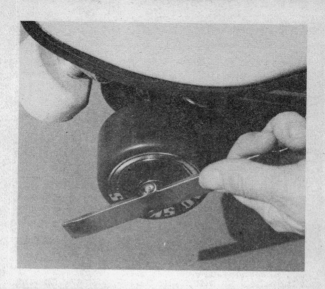

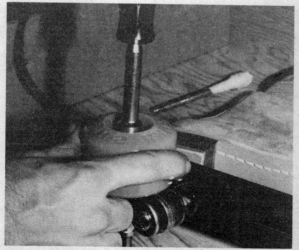

Removal of wheel bearing and wheel.

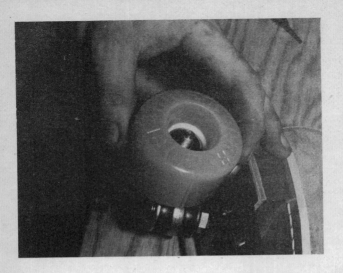

put the wheel unto the axle part-way so the bearing on one side of the wheel just covers the end of the axle. Then, twist the wheel off the axle and the bearing should stay on the axle.

3. Turn the wheel over and do the same to the bearing on the other side.

If these are precision bearings, then they're shielded and you can't clean them as long as the shields are in. If the shields are made of plastic, they're easy to remove. Take a sharp object like a knife and press it between the shield and the inner race of the bearing and pry the shield out. It should come out fairly easily. If the shield is a metal one, it's a bit harder. Do pretty much the same, but pry in one place, then move about a third of the way around the bearing and pry again until the shield pops out. Don't force it. Remove one shield at a time.

4. Pour some solvent into a small can or pyrex dish. Don't use gasoline. Drop the bearings in the solvent. Stir them around until clean. A toothbrush is

Refitting bearing and wheel.

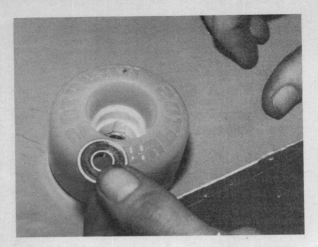

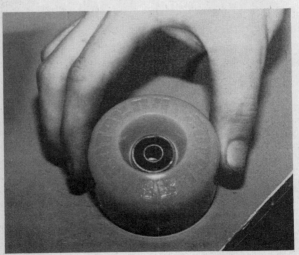

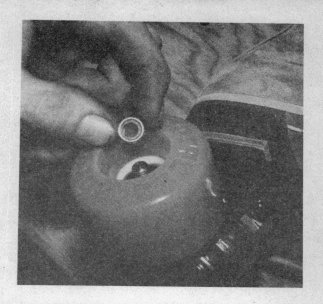

helpful in scrubbing out old grease. Remove the bearings from the solvent and spin. If the tic-tic sound is still there, put the bearings back and rinse some more. When they roll perfectly quiet and smooth, dry on a paper.

5. Using a heavy grease (M-6 put out by Lubrico, or any other heavy grease, heavier than vaseline), pack the bearings. Use your finger or the nozzle of the grease tube to apply. The grease acts like a seal, preventing dirt from reaching the bearings. Caution: Use *very little* grease or it can liquify when it heats up while skating.

6. Replace the bearings and lock in again. Be sure to replace so the open part of the bearing is on the inside of the wheel and the shielded part faces out. Some skaters use WD-40, Triflon (distributed by Powell Corp. which makes Bones Wheels), or Super-Skate spray (distributed by Control Products of Venice,

Adjusting the action.

Ca.) instead of grease to lubricate their bearings. These lubricants make the wheels spin faster. The bearings may burn out in time, but the speed skater, especially, accepts that disadvantage for the added slide.

ADJUSTING SKATE ACTION

Most skates are tested at the factory before shipping. The action is adjusted fairly tight, but not so tight that the cushions bulge. For many skaters, that's fine. To get a sloppy action, just use a skate-key wrench to loosen the action nut about one and a half turns, then turn the lock pin until satisfied. Retighten the action nut.

If you purchase skates which have not been pre-checked before leaving the store, do the following: Check all nuts and bolts to be sure they're tight. Adjust the action nuts as above.

Some skaters think that loose truck action is needed for skateboard park tricks. Not so. Many authorities say a good skater does as well with a snug truck as with a loose one. In fact, a tight truck gives better control.

ROTATING WHEELS

In rinks, most wheels wear evenly, so it's not necessary to rotate them. But, if you regularly drag one of the other skate on an edge, the wheels on that side of the skate will wear more. Instead of wearing flat, they may become rounded, or coned. If that happens, it's good to rotate the wheels like the tires on a car. Just unscrew the axle nut and D-washer and place the coned wheels on the skate which wears normally, or on the opposite side of the same skate.

RUBBER CUSHIONS

Because of truck action, it may be necessary to replace the cushions from time to time. They dry out or squinch down. Loosen the nut. Undo the king pin. Remove the old rubber and replace with new. Then tighten the king pin and nut. The rubber insert where the pivot of the truck goes into the plate may also break down in time. When it does, it's usually on the bottom side. Replacement parts are available at any good rink or skate rental store. Consider switching to urethane cushions when the rubber ones wear out.

TOE STOP

Toe stops usually wear unevenly. That's because skaters favor one foot when stopping. Interchange toe stops left to right, or right to left when worn. That way, the unused stop will get its share of work. Or, rotate the stop by loosening the screw, turning the stop one or two nodules, then tightening the screw again. Check toe stop bolts regularly. They tend to vibrate loose with use and can fall off.

scouting requirements

A MERIT BADGE for roller skating is quite new for scouting. However, with the growing interest in this sport, requirements have been set up by the Boy Scouts of America and Girl Scouts of America for a merit badge.

Many rinks offer six- to eight-week courses to cover the requirements for the badge. Check with your rink. If a class is not available, the rink operator may want to start one if enough scouts are interested.

REQUIREMENTS FOR BOY SCOUT MERIT BADGE

1. Know the following: The general and speed skating safety rules. Be able to discuss the parts and functions of skates.

2. Do the following:

a. Start and stop properly while skating forward and in both directions around the rink.

b. Skate backward first on two feet, then on one foot.

c. Cross the feet in front.

d. Skate a slalom pattern on two feet forward, then on one foot.

e. Shuttle skate.

f. Shoot the duck.

Ready, set, go! A speed trial.

g. The limbo under.
h. The wide spread eagle.
i. Race on a speed track. Start properly, take corners, pass other skaters, pace, and learn the speed skating rules.

The limbo under.

j. The stepover.
k. Spin.
l. Hop, skip, and jump.
m. Dribble a basketball on skates.
n. Push a hockey ball around the rink.
o. Mohawk or two-foot turn.
p. Slalom skate backward on two feet.

Pamphlet #3250 (Skating) is available through Boy Scouts of America, Supply Division, North Brunswick, N.J. 08902, or 1930 North Mannheim Road, Melrose Park, Ill. 60160, or 120 San Gabriel Drive, Sunnyvale, Ca. 94086. The pamphlet includes a short history of roller skating, safety rules and uses of skates, equipment and skate care, and instructions on how to skate.

REQUIREMENTS FOR JUNIOR GIRL SCOUT BADGE—"SKATER"

Junior Girl Scouts (nine to eleven years old, fourth through sixth grades) can now earn a merit badge for roller skating. They must satisfy the following requirements:

1. Tell how to select and care for skates. Explain safety rules for rolling skating. Show how to stop quickly.

2. Using good form, skate forward, backward, to your left, to your right, around corners to the left and then to the right.

3. With a partner, skate forward, backward, and in a dance position.

4. Learn to play and teach one skating game.

5. Practice skating to music and be able to do one dance to music.

6. Explain or show how to give first aid to a skater who is hurt.

7. Read about roller skating. Be able to discuss diet, exercise, and training required for a champion skater. Be able to recognize advanced styles of skating.

8. Help plan and take part in a skating party either indoors or out, *or* make and wear part of a safe skating costume.

CADETTE GIRL SCOUTS

Cadette girl scouts (twelve to fourteen years old, seventh through ninth grades) may earn the Sports Badge

Rounding a corner on a speed track.

for proficiency in roller skating. To qualify for this badge, the scout must be more than a beginner. Among the requirements are:

1. Learn the rules of skating and be able to explain them to others. Practice until you can perform well.

2. Tell about the history and development of roller skating and the countries in which it is popular. Know the types of competition or tournaments connected with it.

3. Know how to select, care for, use, and store your skates.

4. Know the health and safety rules and the proper attire to wear. Show how to give first aid for the type of injury which might occur as a result of skating.

5. Take part in some form of competition. Afterward, analyze and discuss with other participants how you can improve your performance.

6. Help plan and put on a roller skating competition.

7. Be a judge in a competition.

books and magazines about skating

SKATER MAGAZINE. P.O. Box 534, Endicott, N.Y. 13760. $9.50 a year, 6 issues, U.S. or Canada. Covers competition skating nationally and internationally. Profiles on skaters.

SKATE. 7700 A St., Lincoln, Nebr. 68510. $3.00 for 4 issues a year. This is the official magazine of the Roller Skating Rink Operators Association in cooperation with the U.S. Amateur Confederation of Roller Skating. Information for rink operators, competition results, skater profiles, advertising of latest skate apparel and equipment. Concentrates on competitive skating.

ROLLER SKATING MAGAZINE. Box 1028 Dana Point, Ca. 92629. U.S. $7, foreign $10 per year. This is a new magazine. Lots of color photos. Story coverage of outdoor skating scene, such as what's new at skateboard parks, outdoor competitions, profiles of disco skaters, delivery clerks on skates, etc. Lively, colorful with national and international coverage.

(Roller Skating Manuals and Rule Books.) Roller Skating Rink Operators Association. RSROA, 7700 A St., Lincoln, NB 68510, 1973, 9 volumes, $2.00 each:

General Rules
Roller Dance—Part I
Roller Dance—Part II
Roller Speed Skating
Roller Figure Skating
Roller Free Skating
Ball Roller Hockey
Puck Roller Hockey
Tabulation and Scoring

ROLLER HOCKEY (Of Sticks and Skates and City Streets) by Zander Hollander and Steve Clark. Hawthorn Books, New York, 1976. $2.95 paperback.

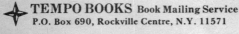